BEAUTIFUL DREAMER

P9-CEG-677

Stephen Collins Foster, 1826–1864. Reprinted from a retouched daguerreotype, courtesy of the Foster Hall Collection, Center for American Music, University of Pittsburgh Library System

BEAUTIFUL DREAMER

The Life of
Stephen Collins Foster

To:
Mr J.P. Cunningham
and family with
Best Wishes,

Ellen Hunter Ulken

This book was printed in the United States of America.

The Cover Art:

The painting on the cover, *Many Happy Days I Squandered*, hangs in the Stephen Foster Museum at the Stephen Foster Folk Culture Center in White Springs, Florida. The artist, Howard Chandler Christy, 1873–1952 (not related to the minstrel singer, E. P. Christy), intended the boy in the picture to represent Stephen and the girl, a friend, in the blithe days of youth. Christie completed the painting in 1950, two years before he died. The title of the painting uses a line from the second verse of "Old Folks at Home." "Many happy days I squandered, many the songs I sung." We have reprinted the painting with permission from the Stephen Foster Folk Culture Center in White Springs from a photo by Priscilla Strozier, Jasper, Florida.

To order additional copies of this book, contact:
Xlibris Corporation
1-888-795-4274
www.Xlibris.com
Orders@Xlibris.com
26233

Contents

The letters are quoted from the biographical references and are italicized. The spelling in the letters is that of the letter writers.

The black dialect has been removed from "Oh! Susanna," "Camptown Races," "Nelly Was a Lady," "Nelly Bly," and "Old Folks at Home." This change respects the sensitivity of readers and does not detract from the meaning or the beauty of the songs.

—A word preceding an asterisk (*) can be found in the glossary.

—Small numbers above the lines (¹) follow direct quotes, the sources of which can be found in the notes.

The subtlest spirit of a nation is expressed through its music—and the music acts reciprocally* on the nation's very soul.

—Walt Whitman

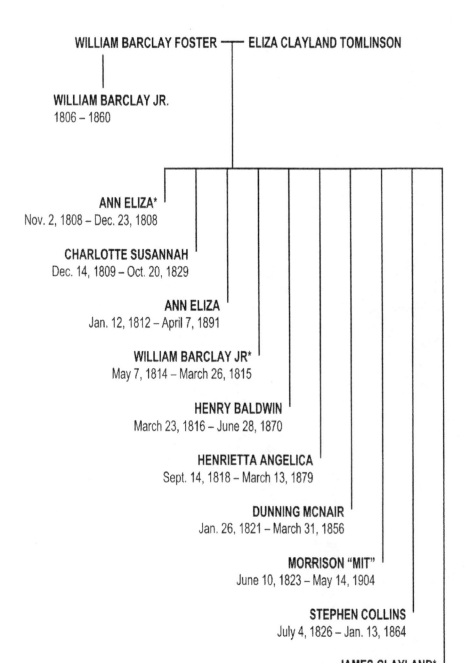

WILLIAM BARCLAY FOSTER —— ELIZA CLAYLAND TOMLINSON

WILLIAM BARCLAY JR.
1806 – 1860

ANN ELIZA*
Nov. 2, 1808 – Dec. 23, 1808

CHARLOTTE SUSANNAH
Dec. 14, 1809 – Oct. 20, 1829

ANN ELIZA
Jan. 12, 1812 – April 7, 1891

WILLIAM BARCLAY JR*
May 7, 1814 – March 26, 1815

HENRY BALDWIN
March 23, 1816 – June 28, 1870

HENRIETTA ANGELICA
Sept. 14, 1818 – March 13, 1879

DUNNING MCNAIR
Jan. 26, 1821 – March 31, 1856

MORRISON "MIT"
June 10, 1823 – May 14, 1904

STEPHEN COLLINS
July 4, 1826 – Jan. 13, 1864

JAMES CLAYLAND*
Feb. 3, 1829 – May 19, 1830

* Died in infancy

Part One

Childhood and Youth

1826-1846

The White Cottage. Reprinted from a sketch by Joseph Muller. Courtesy of the Foster Hall Collection, Center for American Music, University of Pittsburgh Library System

Chapter One

The White Cottage

On the Fourth of July in 1826, the fiftieth anniversary of the signing of the Declaration of Independence, a lively group reveled in a field near the White Cottage, the Foster family home. Stephen Collins Foster was born in the cottage that day while his father, William, as a representative to the Pennsylvania legislature, emceed the ceremonies on the lawn for the nation's birthday party. Fireworks sparkled, banners waved, and cannons boomed so loudly that guests feared the noise would damage the new baby's ears. Friends suggested the baby be named Jefferson Adams because on the day that Stephen was born, John Adams and Thomas Jefferson, the second and third presidents of the United States, both died. But his mother, Eliza, had already decided to name him Stephen Collins to honor their friends, the Collins, whose only son had died at the age of twelve.

A Fourth of July birthday was perfect for this first composer of American popular songs. Stephen Foster would grow up to write the music that felt the pulse of American whimsy and the paradox* of its pain. During his short life, he would watch the great migration to the western frontiers from the bustling river towns of Pittsburgh and Cincinnati, embrace the pleasure of music and theater, mourn the deaths of friends and family members, and struggle with the issues of slavery among a "free people" and a civil war dividing the nation.

Stephen's father, William Barclay Foster Sr, had lived in Pittsburgh since he was sixteen years old. One of its pioneers, he worked there as a merchant and trader when the town was young and small. He met Stephen's mother, Eliza Clayton Tomlinson, while on a trip to Philadelphia where Eliza visited her aunt. Eliza came from a family whose "ladies were distinguished in Baltimore society for their musical and artistic ability."[1] William descended from Irish forebears, and Eliza, from Anglo-American. Eliza and William married in the east in 1807 when he was twenty-eight and she, not quite twenty. They traveled by horseback and wagon through the Allegheny Mountains westward to Pittsburgh.

The Fosters lived in town for a number of years and had several children before buying a large tract of land on the Allegheny River near Pittsburgh. There, they built their home, the White Cottage, keeping some acreage around the house for farmland and a wide view to the river. William B. Foster sold another piece of land to the U.S. government for an arsenal and divided the rest into plots as the town of Lawrenceville.

The great turnpike, one of the roadways connecting east to west, ran past the White Cottage along the Allegheny River. Weary westbound travelers stopped at the Fosters' well to have a drink of cool water and to rest. The railroad had not yet pushed its way across the Allegheny Mountains, so the Ohio and Mississippi rivers remained the nation's main avenues of commerce. Pittsburgh, nestled between the Allegheny and the Monongahela rivers where they join to form the Ohio River, had become an important port and trading center. Coal and iron ore enriched the lands around the city. Smoke and soot spat from the tall chimneys of the iron foundries. Pittsburgh was awash in the noise of blast furnaces and the clanging of blacksmiths, hammering iron into the shapes of useful tools. Glassmaking and boatbuilding were also thriving industries.

Stephen grew up with the sounds and scenes of the rivers. He saw steamboats winding around the river bends and heard their haunting whistles. The fables of river life and the escapades of river men embodied the lore of Pittsburgh.

Brother William was William Sr.'s son by a former relationship. When the boy's mother died and the Fosters' firstborn son died in 1815, Brother William entered the Foster family and was given the name of the dead infant: William B. Foster Jr. This devoted eldest son offered assistance to parents and siblings all of his life. In 1826, the year Stephen was born, Brother William, aged twenty, left home to join an engineering firm.

Eliza Foster gave birth to ten children. Charlotte—the well-loved oldest sister who played piano, sang, and loved music—died when Stephen was three years old while staying with relatives in Kentucky. She had delayed her return home to help care for a young cousin who was ill. The disease that took Charlotte's life, called bilious fever, could have been malaria. (Yellow fever, tuberculosis, cholera, and malaria killed hordes of people in tragic waves and epidemics before the modern age of antibiotics and miracle cures.) Charlotte's death, two months before her twentieth birthday, cast a pall over the entire family for a long time.

Three of Eliza's children died in infancy. One of them, Baby James, died in 1830, making Stephen, almost four years old, the youngest child. Within the space of half a year, Stephen had lost his oldest sister and his youngest brother. We can only imagine the impact of those losses on a three-year-old child.

Of the children who survived, Ann Eliza was born in 1812, Henry in 1816, Henrietta in 1818, Dunning in 1821, Morrison in 1823, and Stephen in 1826. Stephen loved all of his brothers and sisters, but Morrison, nicknamed "Mit," was closest to his own age. Stephen and Mit grew up together, went to school together, shared the same friends and books, and got along well all their lives.

At age two, Stephen already plucked on the strings of Ann Eliza's guitar. He called it his "ittly pizani"—his little piano. In a letter to Brother William, written when Stephen was almost six, his mother notes, "Stevan . . . has a drum and marches about after the old way with a feather in his hat . . . whistling old lang syne . . . There still remains something perfectly original about him."[2] When Stephen was seven years old, mother and son visited a music store in Pittsburgh. Stephen picked up a flageolet—a kind of flute—figured out its notes and fingering, and sounded out a familiar patriotic song to the astonishment of the adults in the store.

In the nineteenth century, girls commonly learned to play piano, guitar, or violin. They received musically centered educations while boys learned trades or professions. Radios and record players had not been invented. If families enjoyed music, they made it themselves or attended church, a concert, or the theater. Fortunately, the Foster family appreciated music and literature, which compensated for the limited formal education the children received. The family spent their evenings singing together and reading aloud. Stephen's father, William Sr., played the violin. Ann Eliza and Henrietta played guitar and wrote poetry. Stephen's mother, Eliza, wrote poetry and penned a memoir of her early years in Pittsburgh. Everyone sang.

Lieve (Olivia Pise), the racially mixed daughter of a French dancing teacher from the West Indies, worked for the Fosters at the White Cottage. Active in her church and in the raising of the young Foster children, she often took Stephen with her to church, the timbers of which reverberated with the interesting sounds of African spirituals and chants. Lieve hummed and sang as she went about her duties at the Fosters'. When no longer indentured*, Lieve left the Foster home, but the children kept her songs alive long after she departed, and her melodies were some of the first that captured Stephen's heart.

The Foster family lived in the White Cottage for only a few years after Stephen's birth. By 1829, due to economic hard times and a scarcity of cash, William Sr. couldn't keep up the mortgage payments. From then on, the family moved frequently: from Allegheny to Pittsburgh to Youngstown and back to Pittsburgh, from boarding house to rented house, or to visit with relatives. Sometimes Stephen stayed with his sister Henrietta, his brother William, or his uncle John Struthers. Wherever they lived, they mourned the loss of their beautiful home on the river. Though Stephen had little experience of the cottage himself, that yearning for a lost home would be expressed repeatedly in his songs.

Chapter Two

Tioga Waltz

Stephen didn't like school. After being called upon to speak in his first kindergarten class, he ran home, yelling all the way. Stephen grasped concepts rapidly and felt confined and stifled in the classroom. He preferred the solitude of the woods and the songs of birds or idling on the riverbanks with his pencils and notebook. He had to go to school, however, and slowly, he adjusted. Stephen and his brother Mit attended the Allegheny Academy in 1834, with other young men from prominent Pittsburgh families. By 1837, when Stephen was eleven years old, the brothers studied with the Reverend Nathan Todd, who told William Sr. that Stephen was the most perfect gentleman he had ever had for a pupil. Later, the boys went to the free school—that is, the public school—in Youngstown, Ohio, under the supervision of their sister Henrietta.

Stephen learned most of his music on his own or from his older sisters. On her guitar, Henrietta taught him all the simple chords his little hands could reach. At various times as he grew up, he also practiced the flute, the clarinet, the piano, and the melodeon.

When he was ten years old, he wrote a letter to his father while visiting Henrietta in Youngstown:

> *My Dear father*
>
> *I wish you to send me a commic songster for you promised to. if I had my pensyl I could rule my paper. or if I had the money to by Black ink But if I had my whistle I would be so taken with it I do not think I would write atall.*
>
> *I remayne your loving son*
>
> *Stephen C. Foster*

"Songsters" provided the 1840s' equivalent to the latest CD of today. These booklets contained the lyrics of the newest popular tunes without musical notes since most people already knew the melodies. Songsters were titled with the first song of its pages or named after minstrel groups or sponsors. The songsters fascinated Stephen, as did the tunes and sketches of the minstrels, the popular entertainment of the era.

The minstrel show comprised a company of performers in "blackface"* who sang songs and made jokes. White and black performers entertained eager audiences. Whites darkened their faces with burnt cork and mimicked black people in jest. A banjo strummed or a fiddler played in concert with the singers. A set of bones tapped together in a rhythmic beat made the sounds of castanets. Sometimes a performer ran a rib up and down the teeth of a dried horse jawbone to make percussion, or someone shook a tambourine.

Stephen and some of his friends performed their own "blackface" shows at home, with Stephen as the star, where the young troupe received much applause and enough pennies to attend the professional performances at the old Pittsburgh Theater. Stephen's attraction for the minstrel music would be at once a pleasure and a source of confusion for him as he grew up. Any subject was fair game for a joke in a minstrel show. Hiding behind the burnt-cork masks, the performers did burlesque* parodies of opera arias and critiqued the American culture. The performances were seen as lowbrow entertainment and insulting to black people. The minstrel shows also insulted women, as male dominance was one of their themes; and they poked fun at authority figures, ethnic groups, and the upper class.

A visit with Henrietta usually included a trip to Uncle Struthers' farm. Stephen loved to visit his elderly uncle, who lived in a log house a few miles from Youngstown, Ohio. John Struthers had grown up on the frontier when Indian uprisings made it necessary to live with a rifle at hand. Stephen amused himself on the farm: watching the animals, just thinking, or listening to the frontier tales of Uncle Struthers. And his uncle enjoyed young Stephen and thought him gifted enough to become "a very great man." Stephen, most comfortable within the realm of his imagination, could drift and dream at Uncle Struthers,' Henrietta wrote in a letter about her young brother. "He never appears to have the least inclination to leave there."[1]

When Stephen was fourteen years old, his eldest brother, William, assumed responsibility for his education. Stephen first enrolled in the Towanda Academy in Towanda, Pennsylvania, where Brother William lived and later in the Athens Academy at Tioga Point, Pennsylvania. Though Stephen stayed to himself at the Athens Academy, his musical and poetic talents required him to participate in school entertainments. For a school exhibition in the Presbyterian Church, he composed *Tioga Waltz*, his first composition, and dedicated it to Frances Welles, who played piano and lived close to the school. Though Frances was older than Stephen, she invited him to practice music at her family's large estate: Tioga Point Farm. Three flutist students—James Forbes, William Warner, and Stephen— performed the piece for an enthusiastic audience on April 1 of 1841.

Stephen boarded with a family in Athens as out-of-town students usually did. Here is a letter of November of 1840 from Stephen in the Athens Academy to Brother William in Towanda:

> *Dear Brother,*
>
> *As Mr. Mitchell is going to start for Towanda today, I thought I would write you a line concerning my studies as he says you will not be here for more than a week.*
>
> *My Philosophy Grammar and Arithmetic not being enough to keep me going I would ask your permission to Study either Latin or Book keeping.*
>
> *I have no place to study in the evenings as the little ones at Mr. Herricks keep such a crying and talking that its imposible to read. There is a good fire place in my room and if you will just say the word I will have a fire in it at nights and learn something. When you come dont forget my waiscoat at the tailors. there are several little articles which I need though I have no room to mention them. I must stop writing as I am very cold.*
>
> *Your affectionate Brother*
> *Stephen*

Brother William had to pay an extra fee to warm the bedroom, but with the fireplace lit, Stephen could practice his music in peace.

Mit described Stephen as slender and not over five feet seven inches tall with small, almost delicate, hands and feet. His most remarkable features were his large deep brown eyes, which "lit up with unusual intelligence." A classmate at the Athens Academy portrayed Stephen with brownish black hair, a well-proportioned face, a square jaw, and dark skin. He appeared to his classmates to be studious and shy with "idle, dreaming ways" and didn't join the other students in sports games.

Stephen's mother, Eliza, was either very sad or very happy, and Stephen inherited this tendency for wide swings in mood. The various moods of his music also extended from happy and silly to melancholy and nostalgic.

Sometime after the spring of 1841, Stephen didn't want to go back to Athens, "that lonely place." Frances Welles, his friend and mentor, had married and moved away from there. He begged to live and study again in Towanda where his brothers Henry and William were living and working. Henry could provide companionship and supervision, argued Stephen, while Brother William was away on business for the Pennsylvania Canal. Brother William gave in and allowed Stephen to stay in Towanda.

In July of 1841—four months later—William and Stephen traveled to Pittsburgh to visit their parents, and the taste of home was so good for the younger brother that he refused to return to Towanda with Brother William. Stephen asked to attend Jefferson College in Canonsburg, Pennsylvania, where his own father had gone in his youth. The older family members agreed. Stephen's father left him at the school in Canonsburg on July 20, 1841.

Four days after his arrival there, Stephen wrote a letter to Brother William. He described the situation at the school, complained of being short on cash, and listed his expenses and when they would be due: "*For Pa has not much more than the means of getting along, I thought I would write you this letter that you might consider over 'the matter.'*" Stephen, aware that Brother William shouldered much of the financial responsibility for the family, thanked his brother for his "unceasing kindness," and signed off.

Three days after writing the letter, Stephen couldn't resist a sudden opportunity to travel to Pittsburgh with a fellow classmate. Seven days after enrolling in the college in Canonsburg, Stephen appeared at home on the doorstep. His mother accepted his return and even said to Brother William, "I shall be almost too lonely without one child with me." [2] His father simply said, "He is a good boy, but I cannot get him to stick at school."[3]

Then fifteen years old, Stephen lived and studied in Pittsburgh. At last, not bound to a schoolroom and school rules, he had time to allow his creative spirit to flourish. Stephen's father said of his son, "His leisure hours are all devoted to musick for which he has a strange talent."[4] The family didn't know how to cope with his talent. They didn't forbid him from pursuing music, but they considered music a distraction from learning a trade that would prepare him for adulthood. Stephen made promises on more than one occasion that he would study by daylight and practice music only during leisure time in the evenings.

He studied the masters of musical composition such as Mozart, Weber, and Beethoven, and became proficient in both French and German.

Chapter Three

Open Thy Lattice Love

Over the winter of 1841, the family lived in a house belonging to Brother William in Allegheny, a suburb of Pittsburgh. Longtime friends occupied other houses in this familiar neighborhood. Morrison, Dunning, and Stephen lived with their parents while brothers William and Henry still worked for the same company in Towanda. Anne Eliza lived with her ever-growing family in Lancaster County, and Henrietta resided in Youngstown, Ohio, with her husband and children.

Stephen and his mother stayed home during the day while the others went off to work. Stephen made music, learned math, and helped in his father's office.

William B. Foster Sr. endured numerous financially uncertain years, at times unemployed and at times having modest-paying political appointments. He had many friends and acquaintances, some in prominent positions, and even when the senior Foster's funds diminished, his optimism stayed constant. In October of 1841, the elder Foster received two job offers at once. One position required a move to Washington, and the other would make him the mayor of Allegheny. In order to remain close to Youngstown, where Henrietta's husband had fallen ill, William Sr. decided to stay at home and take the job of mayor. He sent Henry to Washington to take the clerkship in the Treasury Department.

The spring of 1842 found Eliza Foster visiting Henry in Washington and her relatives on the eastern shore of Maryland. Entertained royally by her relatives, Eliza had a grand trip. Henry, who liked society as much as Stephen did not like it, escorted their mother around Washington and joined her in Maryland where they attended more parties.

Without Eliza, the family felt lonely. Mit described his mother as the heart of the family, "a continual light from heaven." Though at times she regretted their financial situation and the dim prospects of a brighter future,

she felt fortunate that her husband was active in the Temperance Movement.*
(The Washingtonian Temperance Movement, to which William Sr.
belonged, became a sort of precursor to Alcoholics Anonymous.) Eliza
received comfort from her faith in God. A religious person, she regularly
conducted spontaneous family prayer sessions.

After the children grew up, they made contributions to the household
even if they were not living at home. Brother William saved all the letters
he got from his parents; the letters contained acknowledgments for
contributions he had made by mail and references to money gifts from
Dunning as well. The family members—a loyal, close-knit group—each
felt responsible for the welfare of the others.

Mit traveled the river as a cotton buyer for Pollard McCormick's mill, but
when at home on days off, he attended plays and musicals with Stephen.
Inspired by the music he heard in the theaters and the music swimming in his
head, Stephen often sat at the piano, arranging and improvising. In December
1844, George Willig, of Philadelphia, published Stephen's first song, "Open
Thy Lattice Love." Stephen wrote the music to a poem by George Pope Morris
and dedicated the song to his friend Susan Pentland, of Pittsburgh.
Unfortunately for Stephen, the publisher misprinted his initials as L. C. Foster!

Printing was a time-consuming and intricate process in the nineteenth
century. The type had to be set by hand or engraved onto metal plates in
preparation for the work of the printing press. If a mistake occurred, it
stayed until new plates were prepared. The absence of computers, in
Stephen's day, meant no quick deletions and easy corrections with the
punch of a typewriter key.

Mit got Stephen his first paid job at Mr. McCormick's New Hope
Warehouse, checking cotton bales as they were transported from the wharf
into the building. Stephen watched the activities along the river and listened
to the rhythmical singing of the workers who loaded and off-loaded the
boats. He heard the cadence of the stevedores'* songs and felt the spirit of
their music.

Stephen and Mit belonged to a young men's club called the Knights
of the Square Table, which formed in 1845. Stephen wrote his first
songs for the group and often had the "Knights" sing his music. He
wrote a poem for the members, a humorous description of their crowd,
called "The Five Nice Young Men," which demonstrates Stephen's great
sense of fun. The following is a sample from Stephen's poem about his
best friend Charles Shiras:

First, there's Charlie the elder, the Sunday-School teacher,
Who laughs with a groan,
In an unearthly tone,
Without moving a bone
Or a feature.

He followed with funny verses about "Charlie the younger" and three other members of the group.

The Knights of the Square Table met twice a week at the Fosters' home and sang the popular music of the day. The young men sometimes invited their women friends over to join them in singing Stephen's songs. The Keller girls lived close by, and the chorus occasionally practiced at their house. In 1846, at the age of twenty, Stephen dedicated a song to Mary Keller called "There's a Good Time Coming." Two months later, Mary died, and Stephen wrote another song in her honor for her sister Rachel, "Where Is Thy Spirit, Mary?" published after Stephen's death. For the "Knights," Stephen wrote "Lou'siana Belle," and they liked it so much he came to the next meeting with "Old Uncle Ned."

The five "nice young men."

First, there's Charley the elder, the sunday-school teacher,
  Who laughs with a groan,
  In an unearthly tone,
  Without moving a bone
  Or a feature.

Then Charley the younger, the Illinois screecher,
  Who never gets mad,
  But always seems glad,
  While others are sad;
Though his face is so long that it would'nt look bad
  On a methodist preacher.

There's Andy, who used to be great on a spree,
Whose duets (as he calls them) all fit to a T.
  But people do tell us
  He's got just as jealous
  Of Latimer as he can be.
  They say that he wishes
  The sharks and the fishes
Would catch him and eat him when he gets out to sea.

And Bob, that smokes seventeen tobies a day,—
He's liberal, however, and gives some away.
  Bob's been to college
  Picking up knowledge
But now he's got home and I hope he will stay.

We will wind up with Harvey, the fluffer, the gay.
He can play on the fiddle (or thinks he can play)
  Harvey's mind
  Is inclined
  To all that's refined,
  With a count'nance so bright
  That it rivals the light
Of the sun that now cheers us in this sweet month of May.

— Pittsburgh —
— May 6, 1845 —

By Stephen C Foster —

Stephen's poem of "The Five Nice Young Men" written by his own hand. Courtesy of the Foster Hall Collection, Center for American Music, University of Pittsburgh Library System

Part Two

Cincinnati

1846-1850

Title page of sheet music for "Oh! Susanna." Courtesy of the Foster Hall Collection, Center for American Music, University of Pittsburgh Library System

Chapter Four

Oh! Susanna

Stephen had reached the age of twenty in 1846 and needed to choose an occupation. His family didn't consider songwriting a reasonable choice. Songwriters of that era earned a steady income in their "real" jobs as blacksmiths, lawyers, teachers, and storekeepers. Taking a church position as music director would have been an acceptable way to pursue a musical career and earn a living at the same time, but Stephen didn't consider that option, as far as is known. Though his family were devoted Episcopalians, and Stephen wrote hymns for Sunday school and church during the last years of his life, the free-spirited Stephen wouldn't be bound by the demands of a vocation, which would take him out of his own world and away from his own music.

He expressed interest in the Naval Academy, perhaps dreaming of a seaman's life, and the family tried to get him an appointment to the United States Military Academy at West Point, New York, where they had some contacts. When this attempt failed, the parents asked Dunning to put Stephen to work in Cincinnati. Dunning had worked as a clerk on a steamboat from 1840 to 1846, and then joined Archibald Irwin, as Irwin and Foster, commission merchants on Cassily's Row.

At the age of twenty, Stephen cruised down the Ohio River to Cincinnati to be a bookkeeper in his brother's company, a better alternative than military service. In the schoolrooms of his youth, he had shown his aversion to the structure and rules that typify military life.

Ohio was a free state* and Cincinnati, an important station on the Underground Railroad*, the route for smuggling slaves to Canada and freedom. Across the river lay Kentucky, a slave state.

Long before Stephen moved to Cincinnati, Charlotte had described it as "the most beautiful city in western country," and long after he moved back to Pittsburgh, he told his daughter, Marion, that the Cincinnati years had been the happiest of his life.

Irwin and Foster competed with several other companies for passenger and freight trade, and they sold used boats. Their offices faced the river, and every day, Stephen felt the energy of the waterfront activities. He could see the stevedores* shift the cargo to and from the steamboats and hear their humming, the burden of hard work made lighter with the singing. The riverside revealed a colorful blending of the country's multiethnic people.

Commerce and society mixed and mingled among the river cities of Pittsburgh, Louisville, and Cincinnati. When Stephen arrived in Cincinnati, he already knew a number of people who lived there. Stephen and Dunning lived at Jane Griffen's boarding house, within easy walking distance to work. Near the boarding house stood a number of music stores, selling pianos, violins, wind instruments, and an abundance of sheet music. Peters and Fields, a large music publishing house located in the city, owned four music presses and two lithographic* presses.

Plays, concerts, and minstrel shows were staged in the various theaters around town, and Stephen attended them all. Shires Garden, the Melodeon, and the National Theater drew large audiences, the latter being the usual house for performing Shakespearean plays.

Christy's Minstrels, one of the best-known minstrel troupes of the day, had engagements in Cincinnati in November of 1846 and in August of 1847. The Sable Harmonists appeared frequently during 1846 through 1849. The Empire Minstrels, Danny Rice, and Nelson Kneass' Great Original Sable Harmonists also appeared in Cincinnati during Stephen's years there. He met many of the performers and wrote songs for them.

Cincinnati, a center for industry and trade, exhibited a hectic assortment of productive activity. Nicknamed Porkopolis, herds of hogs plodded Cincinnati's streets headed for slaughter and shipping to other destinations. Wagons and carts filled the streets, bringing produce from the farms to sell in town or to ship to other ports by steamboat. Off-loaded and reloaded, the same wagons hauled supplies back to the farms. Stagecoaches rumbled through town, bringing travelers and businessmen. Riverfronts bustled with traffic: workers loading and off-loading the boats, boats docking and steaming off again, leaving some passengers at the dock and taking others away.

In 1849, the heyday of the gold rush, thousands of people came through town by wagon train. Stagecoaches brought thousands more to ride the steamboats as far as Independence, Missouri, for the long trek west. (Both the Santa Fe and the Oregon trails originated in Independence.) Danger accompanied steamboats and river life in the early days. Boilers sometimes exploded, causing injury and death, and snags in the river channels caused accidents and more death. When Zachary Taylor* campaigned for the presidency in 1848, he promised federal money to improve the ports and harbors.

Dunning enlisted as a soldier in the Mexican War and left Cincinnati in June of 1847 for a one-year enlistment. Stephen held down the Foster side of the office and learned to be a good bookkeeper. He also enjoyed an active social life and met many of the distinguished writers and concert artists in the city.

While Dunning fought in the Mexican War, Stephen created his first great songwriting success—a polka, the newest dance step from Paris. The beat may have been Parisian, but the song was American.

Oh! Susanna

I come from Alabama
With my banjo on my knee;
I'm goin' to Lou'siana
My true love for to see.
It rained all night the day I left,
The weather it was dry,
The sun so hot I froze to death,
Susanna, don't you cry.

Chorus

Oh! Susanna,
Do not cry for me;
I come from Alabama,
With my banjo on my knee.

Nelson Kneass directed the musical productions at the Andrew's Eagle Ice-Cream Saloon in Pittsburgh where "Oh! Susanna" was originally performed. Mit had entered Stephen's song into a contest there, and though—ironically—it didn't win the contest, it became the greatest hit the world had ever known. "Oh! Susanna" spread like a rushing wind among the towns along the rivers. The minstrels took it to the cities in the east, and the pioneers and gold miners took it to the west, sometimes with altered lyrics. From the Atlantic to the Pacific, banjos rang with "Oh! Susanna."

Everyone could sing this whimsical song. Even the slaves escaping through the Underground Railroad* to Canada sang the tune with words of freedom in their verses:

> O, righteous Father
> Wilt thou not pity me
> And aid me on to Canada
> Where fugitives are free?

The second verse of "Oh! Susanna" contains racially offensive words, so it must have pleased Martin Delaney, an active abolitionist, to substitute the above words for the existing ones. Sojourner Truth, the first black woman orator to speak out against slavery, used the melody for her emancipation poems. Eventually, the song's popularity spread around the globe. For Stephen, the success of "Oh! Susanna" was the proof he needed that he could earn his living writing songs.

Unfortunately, the composer had not anticipated his first big hit. Stephen gave so many copies of "Susanna" away that some arrangements floated around without his name. There was no copyright* law in place to protect a work prior to its being published. Whoever presented a work for copyright first could take out the copyright. (Mit once appeared at the courthouse to get the copyright for one of Stephen's songs, only to find Kneass there for the same purpose with the same Foster song— so confusing and unfair was the situation.) Twenty editions, each different, were being printed of "Oh! Susanna," most of them without Stephen's name, so he didn't earn much from his success. Royalties comprised the few cents the publisher paid to the composer for each piece of sheet music sold, the only income composers received for their works. If they sold their pieces outright, royalties were waived. The publisher W. C. Peters eventually earned thousands of dollars from "Oh! Susanna" but paid Stephen only one hundred dollars.

Dunning returned from the Mexican War weak with fever and a cough. At that time, soldiers suffered more commonly from diseases than from battle wounds. Relapses of his illness would plague Dunning over the rest of his short life.

Stephen's friendship with Jane McDowell, his future wife, started while he was working in Cincinnati. Jane had been born on December 10, 1829, to Scotch-Irish pioneer parents. Jane's father, Dr. Andrew N. McDowell, a prominent Pittsburgh physician and businessman, died suddenly in 1849, leaving a wife and six daughters. Jane's family life overflowed with love and prosperity, but in an era when men earned the money, financial difficulties loomed ahead for this large family of girls.

Mrs. McDowell and her daughters lived in Pittsburgh, but Jane traveled to Cincinnati to visit their friends, the Stewarts. When Stephen and Dunning stopped by to see her, Stephen admired Jane's beauty, her long reddish brown hair, and her fun-loving disposition.

Mit, Dunning, and Stephen were now the unwed children of the family, but they attended the weddings of three boyhood friends during the summer of 1849, two of them Knights of the Square Table. All of the sons, including William, came to Pittsburgh for the parties, celebrations, and reunions with family members. On his way back to Cincinnati, Stephen visited his sister Henrietta and her family in Youngstown. Henrietta's first husband had died of tuberculosis, and she had remarried.

In Cincinnati, more than nine thousand people died of cholera during the summer of 1849, and during the following winter, ten thousand fell ill with smallpox. Hardly a household in the city was untouched by death. Fortunately, Dunning and Stephen escaped both diseases, though Dunning had already contracted tuberculosis during his service in the Mexican War; and Stephen developed a "fever and ague" during the summer of 1849, most likely malaria or tuberculosis, and endured recurring episodes of this febrile* illness throughout his life.

At twenty-three years of age, Stephen concluded his Cincinnati phase. He published "Nelly Was a Lady" in July of 1849. The song is an example of Stephen's respectful treatment of black people. He paints a picture of a happy marriage between Nelly and her devoted husband and shows marriage as an important institution in black society. He presents black people as thinking, feeling, worthy human beings, and describes Nelly as a lady, a term reserved, at that time, for upper-class white women. What follows are three (of the five) verses of "Nelly Was a Lady":

Nelly Was a Lady

Down on the Mississippi floating,
Long time I travel on the way,
All night the cottonwood* a-toting,
Sing for my true love all the day

Chorus

Nelly was a lady,
Last night she died.
Toll the bell for lovely Nell,
My dark Virginia bride.

Now I'm unhappy and I'm weeping,
Can't tote the cottonwood* no more;
Last night, while Nelly was a-sleeping,
Death came a-knocking at the door.

Down in the meadow 'mong de clover,
Walk with my Nelly by my side;
Now all them happy days are over,
Farewell, my dark Virginia bride.

Stephen published "Summer Longings" in November of 1849 and signed contracts with publishers Firth, Pond & Company of New York and F. D. Benteen, of Baltimore, to secure a percentage of royalties for future compositions. He prepared himself for a career move that would satisfy the creative and musical forces within him and that would take him back to his beloved Pittsburgh.

Part Three

Pittsburgh

1850-1860

Chapter Five

Camptown Races

Armed with the success of "Oh! Susanna," the youngest Foster decided to make his living writing songs. He returned to Allegheny in February of 1850 with the encouragement of Henry Kleber, who had been Stephen's musical mentor during his adolescent years. Kleber, an accomplished musician and composer himself, taught piano and voice, and owned a music store in Pittsburgh, "The Sign of the Golden Harp."

On April 22, 1850, the Fosters moved into another comfortable house belonging to Brother William in Allegheny City, a suburb of Pittsburgh on the northern side of the Allegheny River. A hallway divided the house downstairs. One parlor led to another, front to back, on one side of the hall; and the dining room, with its cheerful fireplace, fronted the kitchen on the other. Living there were Eliza and William Sr.; Mit; Stephen; the household helpers; Henry; his wife, Mary; and their daughter, Birdie.

William B. Foster Sr. worked as a soldier's agent in Pittsburgh in charge of pensions and land grants.

When Zachary Taylor took office as the president of the United States in 1849, the Democratic appointments in Washington came to an end, and Henry returned to Pittsburgh and found a job with the Pittsburgh-Steubenville Railroad Company, which later became the Panhandle Railroad Company. Henry and Mary's little daughter, Birdie, was the joy of the household and Eliza's favorite.

Mit spent more time with real estate and the iron and steel industries because the cotton mills no longer prospered. The Pennsylvania legislature had passed a law, prohibiting companies from making their employees work more than ten hours a day. Local mills could no longer compete with those to the South where workers could produce fourteen-hour days. When the mills closed, hard times followed for many who lost their jobs, and families struggled to pay the bills.

The Klebers lived on Sandusky Street, a short pleasant neighborhood walk from the Foster residence on the East Common. Stephen made the walk often and worked closely with Henry Kleber who admired Stephen and shared his musical interests. When the Kleber brothers' new music store opened in 1850, Stephen Foster's sheet music covered the display racks.

Stephen saw Jane McDowell often. The social code of the day prescribed certain times that were proper for visiting. Stephen's handsome rival, Richard Cowan, once appeared at the McDowell doorstep to visit Jane on the same evening that Stephen came to call. Stephen buried his face in a book while Richard visited. At the dot of 10:30 p.m., when the customary time for calling ended, the accomplished Richard Cowan got up to leave, and Stephen stayed behind. Jane didn't know yet which gentleman she preferred, but she didn't have much time to think about it, for Stephen said to her,

"And now, Miss. Jane, I want your answer. Is it yes? Or is it no?" Three months later, Jane and Stephen were married. Jane's sister Agnes McDowell wrote the details to another sister who couldn't attend:

> Jane is really married, and can it be possible. It seems so strange to me that she is married and gone, I can not realize it still, and the wedding over. Jane and Stephen F were pretty much frightened. Steve quite pale. They each had to repeat some part of the ceremony after Mr. Lyman, which made it, I think rather embarrassing. Jane repeated her part in a different kind of a voice altogether from her usual tone of voice. It was owing to her strain. She looked very sweet, her weding dress fit her beautifully, gloves and gaiters* to match her dress, very pretty pair of cuffs and collar. Steven looked very nicely. I was bridesmaid and Morrison groomsman.

Agnes went on to describe the reception and enclosed some wedding cake with the letter, "to dream on." The marriage took place in the Trinity Episcopal Church on July 22, 1850. The newlyweds left for Baltimore and New York on the same day, mixing their honeymoon trip with business. Stephen wanted to meet with his publishers.

Six weeks later, they were back in Allegheny, living with the family on the East Common: father, mother, Mit, Henry and family, Stephen, and Jane. It was a happy time. Stephen had a back room upstairs furnished with piano, chair, lounge, music rack, and table. He worked with the door closed and discouraged interruptions. Stephen, usually gentle and warmhearted, became annoyed with anyone who disturbed his work.

Fourteen of Stephen's songs were published before his wedding day and five more between the wedding day and January of 1851. The most successful were "Nelly Bly" and "Camptown Races."

One evening, the Knights of the Square Table stood on the porch of the Woods family and serenaded the Woods and the McDowells across the way. The housekeeper for the Woods family came outside to listen to the music. Stephen asked about her and discovered her name: Nelly Bly. When the singers were invited inside, Stephen sat at the Woods' piano and wrote the song on the spot, with nearly the same words as the published version. Nelly Bly, the daughter of a former slave, lived to old age, always grateful that Stephen had written a song to her.

Nelly Bly

Nelly Bly! Nelly Bly! Bring the broom along,
We'll sweep the kitchen clean, my dear, and have a little song.
Poke the wood, my lady love, and make the fire burn,
And while I take the banjo down, just give the mush a turn.

Chorus

Heigh, Nelly! Ho, Nelly! Listen, love, to me,
I'll sing for you, play for you, a dulcem melody.
Heigh, Nelly! Ho, Nelly! Listen, love, to me,
I'll sing for you, play for you, a dulcem melody.

A journalist of that era took the pen name of Nellie Bly from the Foster song. Elizabeth Cochrane Seaman, born near Pittsburgh, wrote first for the *Pittsburgh Dispatch*, then for the *New York World*. She pretended insanity to gain hospitalization and the opportunity to observe and expose cruel treatment of mental patients. Reforms resulted. In another journalistic and humanitarian effort, she got herself jailed for thievery and wrote of the brutal treatment of prisoners. In 1889, the *New York World* sent her on a trip around the world to outdo Phileas Fogg, the character in the Jules Verne novel *Around the World in Eighty Days*. She completed her trip by ship, train, donkey, and handcart in 72 days, 6 hours, and 11 minutes.

"Camptown Races," a comic song about betting on the racehorses, featured percussionists tapping their bones to sound like the clippety-clop of trotting horses. This frolicking tune spread out across the nation with the speed of a sprinting stallion.

Camptown Races

The Camptown ladies sing this song,
Doo-dah! Doo-dah!
The Camptown race track five miles long,
Oh! doo-dah-day!
I come down there with my hat caved in
Doo-dah! doo-dah!
I go back home with a pocket full of tin,
Oh! doo-dah-day!

Chorus

Goin' to run all night!
Goin' to run all day!
I'll bet my money on the bobtail nag,
Somebody bet on the bay.

E. P. Christy's name appeared on the title page of the song as a performer. Christy, a minstrel singer, conducted a famous musical group. Stephen felt a conflict, Should he write for the minstrel stage, and if so, should he sell the music straight to the performers who rapidly brought the songs to the performance stage and paid a better fee than the publishers did? The songs written for the minstrel shows were called Ethiopian melodies. Stephen wanted to be accepted as a composer of refined songs and feared he would be associated with coarse, lowlife entertainment by writing for the minstrels. At the same time, he felt drawn to the music of the minstrels for the sheer fun of it, and he experienced an economic incentive. Stephen earned as much as ten times more money from the minstrel songs than from the parlor songs.

Stephen saw Christy as a catalyst for the spread of his music's popularity, for Christy attracted large crowds everywhere he performed. Foster was right. Christy helped to make him famous. Christy, who employed his own family members in his troupe, agreed with Foster on refining the minstrel music for a more dignified audience. Foster worked face-to-face with other minstrel groups, but he and Christy conducted their business by mail. There is no proof that they actually met or that Foster ever attended one of Christy's shows. But probably he did since Christy performed in Cincinnati while Foster lived there.

William B. Foster Sr. had a stroke in April of 1851, disturbing the family tranquility. Though his mind suffered no damage, he sustained partial paralysis and had to live within the walls and windows of his bedroom for the rest of his life. To give the others more space, Henry, Mary, and Birdie moved into a separate house.

Marion, the only child of Stephen and Jane, was born within a few days of William Sr.'s stroke. Stephen helped in the sickroom and the nursery, but he needed privacy for his songwriting. He rented a studio, set up a piano there, and went to and from work on a daily basis. He began using a leather-bound sketchbook for composing lyrics for the songs he would write over the next ten years. The book still exists and can be seen in the Stephen Foster Museum in Pittsburgh. He also kept a complete accounting book for that period, which survives today, in which he meticulously listed the earnings from the songs he wrote and tracked expenditures.

In August of 1851, Stephen and Jane moved to the McDowell home for several months, though Stephen went to see his father every day. William Sr. was no better. He could move his hands, but his legs were limp, and he had to be lifted into an easy chair to sit by the window.

Five songsters were issued in Philadelphia in November of 1851 by Fisher and Brothers, each with a Foster melody in the title: the "Nelly Bly Songster," the "Oh Boys, Carry Me Along Songster," the "Way Down in Ca-i-ro Songster," the "Ring the Banjo Songster," and the "Dolcy Jones Songster."

Foster had sent the manuscript of "Oh Boys, Carry Me 'Long" to E. P. Christy who agreed to pay ten dollars for the privilege of bringing the song to the public first. In a letter, Foster gave Christy instructions on how the song should be sung: "Remember it should be sung in a pathetic, not a comic style." Foster gave more advice: to have it sung in the key of G, to use a tenor voice whose range extends to G, and to keep the harmony as he wrote it. He also asked Christy to have the troupe well practiced before bringing the song to the public.

Stephen depended on Mit and Eliza—especially Eliza, who also had a way with words—to review and critique his lyrics and relied on friends from the neighborhood chorus to practice and sound out his melodies before he took them to the publishers. Susan Pentland and Jessie Lightner, singing in fine harmony, offered memorable performances of the duets in particular.

Title page of sheet music, "Old Folks at Home." Courtesy of the Foster Hall Collection, Center for American Music, University of Pittsburgh Library System

Chapter Six

Old Folks at Home

Stephen wandered into Mit's office one day, looking for the name of a Southern river with two syllables that sounded better than Peedee (a river in North Carolina) for his current composition. Together, they opened the atlas and discussed possibilities. When Mit found the Suwannee, Stephen shortened it to "Swanee," wrote it down, and walked out of the office. In the original manuscript of "Old Folks at Home," you can see where the Peedee River is crossed out and the name Swanee inserted. "Way Down upon the Swanee River," or "Old Folks at Home," became one of his most popular creations. In this ideal unity of melody and rhyme, Stephen captures the nostalgia of childhood and the sweetness of home that, despite its use of black dialect*, transcends race and roots. With this effort, he had brought an Ethiopian melody into the respectable parlor.

Old Folks at Home

Way down upon the Swanee River
Far, far away,
There's where my heart is turning ever,
There's where the old folks stay.
All up and down the whole creation,
Sadly I roam,
Still longing for the old plantation,
And for the old folks at home.

Chorus
All the world is sad and dreary,
Ev'rywhere I roam,
Oh ladies how my heart grows weary,

Far from the old folks at home.

The famous piano performer Louis Moreau Gottschalk used a medley of Foster songs including "Old Folks" in his grand national symphony called *National Glory*. Anton Dvorak, the Czech composer, conducted his own arrangement of "Old Folks." When the flamboyant French maestro Louis Jullien arrived in New York City in the summer of 1853, he hired extra members for his enormous orchestra and introduced *American Quadrille*, a symphony whose third movement's theme was "Old Folks at Home." Decades later, Irving Berlin (composer of "Easter Parade," "White Christmas," and "God Bless America") and George Gershwin (composer of *Rhapsody in Blue* and *Porgy and Bess*) both borrowed "Swanee River" phrases to jazz up their own compositions. Berlin had a portrait of Stephen Foster on his office wall. Ray Charles recorded his own "Swanee River Rock."

Notice the wording on the title page of the song:

OLD FOLKS AT HOME
Ethiopian Melody
As sung by
Christy's Minstrels
Written and composed by
E. P. Christy

Not realizing its potential, Stephen sold to E. P. Christy the right to list himself as author of "Old Folks at Home." Stephen did get royalties from it; and eventually, everyone knew he wrote it, but his name did not appear on the sheet music. Stephen had long been under an arrangement with Christy that for a sum of ten dollars per song, "as sung by E. P. Christy" would appear on the title pages of the plantation songs, along with the composer's name, but this was the first time Foster had sold him a song outright. Within a short period of time, Stephen appealed to Christy by letter, requesting his permission to be allowed to reclaim "Old Folks." "I want to establish my name as the best Ethiopian songwriter," he said in his letter to Christy, and he went on to explain his discovery: that the joy in writing the songs was the pride of their ownership. He intended to further refine the plantation melodies and reinstate his name to all future works. But Christy refused to give up his rights to "Old Folks at Home." In fact, he scrawled across the back of the letter—Christy saved his letters from Foster—the words "vacillating skunk." Not until Mit renewed the copyright in 1879, for the benefit of Stephen's widow and daughter, did Stephen's name appear on the title page.

Waves of tourists traveled to Florida, longing to see the "Swanee River," made famous by Stephen's song. "Old Folks at Home" has served as the state song of Florida since 1935. A memorial to Stephen Foster in White Springs, Florida, includes a museum containing diorama exhibits of scenes from his songs and the world's largest carillon bell tower, chiming his best melodies. The museum and the bell tower lie in a tree-shaded park along the Suwannee River, though our composer saw the river only in his dreams.

The Stephen Foster Folk Culture Center State Park in White Springs is the gathering place for an annual folk festival each May. For three days, Florida celebrates its heritage with music, dance, arts, crafts, and stories. May of 2003 marked one-half century of festivals on the Suwannee River, fifty festivals at Stephen Foster's memorial since 1953.

East Coast composers continued to imitate their European forebears while Stephen, growing up west of the Allegheny Mountains and isolated from his professional peers, wrote music and lyrics with a "western" essence. By infusing the zest of river life and a flavor of black music into his songs, he created an original American sound.

Black music in America has evolved from the spiritual and minstrel songs of the 1800s to ragtime, blues, and jazz of the 1900s. People are fascinated with the soulful quality in the music, the beat, and the opportunities for syncopation* and improvisation. Black music is heard in rock and roll and mixtures of rock music with Caribbean Island music or with country and western or rap. Two centuries of integrating and mixing these various influences have defined American popular music of today. Stephen Foster pioneered this blending of sounds and rhythms.

The twenty to thirty "plantation songs," first called "Ethiopian songs," represented a small portion of Stephen's total lifetime creation of some two hundred pieces. He devoted much more time to the composition of English "airs" or parlor songs, songs for the concert stage, or those in the tradition of Irish and English popular and folk songs. Though his plantation songs relate to black music, they derive, stylistically, from traditional English folk song.

Stephen wanted recognition as a writer of refined compositions, socially and musically correct. "He needed acceptance for what he was writing by the highest cultured taste in this country." [1]

Title page of sheet music, "Old Kentucky Home." Courtesy of the Foster Hall Collection, Center for American Music, University of Pittsburgh Library System

Chapter Seven

Old Kentucky Home

On February 20, 1852, Stephen and Jane boarded a steamboat bound for the Mardi Gras celebration in New Orleans. The round-trip cruise on the Ohio and Mississippi rivers would take a month. Dunning owned and captained the side-wheeler *James Millingar*, and the passengers included some of the Fosters' best friends.

During the daytime, they lounged on the decks of the boat, watching the river traffic and admiring the scenery beyond the riverbanks. Plantation houses with columns and galleries stood at random intervals along the Mississippi River, commanding the vast and fallow farmlands. Oak trees laden with Spanish moss shaded the gardens around the houses, where children tumbled and played. Laborers torched the cotton fields beyond, in preparation for the spring planting, while plants in the unburned fields showed blotches of snowy tufts left over from the harvest.

By moonlight, the travelers broke the silence of the river night and the noise of the steam engine by singing the songs in which Stephen had already described the pastoral landscape surrounding them. This would be the only trip of Stephen's lifetime to take him south of Kentucky.

Stephen may have visited "Federal Hill," the Rowan estate in Bardstown, Kentucky, during the river trip. The Rowan family, relatives of the Fosters, had entertained Stephen's sister Charlotte there, shortly before she died. Proof exists that Stephen saw the place—the boat docked in Louisville, a short trip by coach to Bardstown—and certainly, the Rowans would have welcomed Stephen there. Susan Pentland (Mrs. Andrew Robinson), who traveled with the Fosters on the steamboat, said that Stephen went to Bardstown on the trip, and Mit vouched that Stephen had been an "occasional visitor" at Federal Hill.

Kentuckians believe the house inspired Stephen's song "My Old Kentucky Home Good-Night." He may have conjured up visions of the fine old plantation as he wrote, but "my lady" in the lyric is the lady of the slave cabin and not of the big house. And the "Kentucky Home" is the home of the slave, not the master. A best-selling book provided the impetus for writing the song.

My Old Kentucky Home Good-Night

The sun shines bright in the old Kentucky home,
Tis summer, we're carefree and gay*,
The corn top's ripe and the meadow's in the bloom,
While the birds make music all the day,
The young folks roll on the little cabin floor,
All merry, all happy and bright:
By'n by Hard Times comes a-knocking at the door,
Then my old Kentucky Home, Good night!

Chorus

Weep no more my lady,
Oh! weep no more today !
We will sing one song
For the old Kentucky Home,
For the old Kentucky Home, far away.

Harriet Beecher Stowe published *Uncle Tom's Cabin* on March 20, 1852, the day before the steamboat party returned to Pittsburgh. The book took the country by storm. By May 1, in Pittsburgh alone, shoppers had cleared the bookstores of twenty thousand copies. Stowe depicted the misery of slavery with such clarity and drama that many who read the book realized, for the first time, the cruelty of slave owners who divided slave families through sales. After losing spouses and children at auction sales, slaves suffered for the rest of their lives in sadness and longing. Children, sometimes sold separately to the highest bidder, found themselves in unfamiliar, sometimes harsher, environments, bereft of siblings and consoling parents.

Stowe's book exposed the climate of the country under the Fugitive Slave Law*. As a result of her criticism, the divisions and differences between the North and the South intensified, and many Southerners despised Stowe after her book gripped the nation.

Several dramas came from the story. Music and song accompanied the stage performances. Stephen wrote "My Old Kentucky Home, Good-Night" originally as a song sympathetic to Uncle Tom, one of the featured characters in Stowe's book and the personification of the loyal slave. Several other composers wrote Uncle Tom songs, none of which survive today. In Stephen's sketchbook, the song is seen first as "Poor Uncle Tom Good-Night." But before he finished it, Foster "dropped the blackface dialect* almost entirely . . . he eliminated the references to Uncle Tom, freeing the song from the novel, its politics, and its period, and thereby evoking nearly timeless and universal emotions about losing one's family, home, and childhood."[1] Stephen probably wrote it in 1852 and had it published in 1853.

Frederick Douglass, the black activist /abolitionist, liked the song. He thought it evoked sympathy for the abolitionist cause.

Though she did not authorize the use of *Uncle Tom's Cabin* for the theater productions and did not earn a penny from them, the dramatizations of Harriet Beecher Stowe's story swept the country, often accompanied by Foster songs. The sadness of the story matched the melancholy of the composer's music.

"My Old Kentucky Home" not only survived, but it became the state song of Kentucky. Kentuckians liked it so much they designed their 2001 commemorative quarter-dollar coin with the logo "My Old Kentucky Home" and included the Bardstown plantation house and a racehorse on the coin's face. The beloved Foster song is played yearly at the opening of the famous Kentucky Derby horse race.

A memorial to Stephen Foster exists in Bardstown at the Rowan family mansion. Each summer, in an outdoor amphitheater, actors and singers perform a musical tribute to Foster for hundreds of tourists over a two-month period— nightly except Mondays—at My Old Kentucky Home State Park.

The tracks of the Pennsylvania Railroad reached Pittsburgh on December 11, 1852. It was William B. Foster Jr.'s time to celebrate. Brother William had engineered the blasting of the railway bed along the banks of the Juniata River, investing years of planning, patience, and work to accomplish the task. William Jr. and his wife, Elizabeth, and children were aboard the first train to connect the eastern seaboard with Pittsburgh, the Smoky City west of the Allegheny Mountains. An enthusiastic crowd, including a number of Fosters, awaited the arrival of the little train at the temporary station on Liberty and Twelfth streets.

Before the railroad, it had been a four-day journey, but Stephen could now travel to his publishers in New York in less than one day.

Chapter Eight

Old Dog Tray

"Old Dog Tray" appeared as Foster's American Melody no. 21, Stephen's first hit song not written in black dialect* or about the South. Stephen played a few bars of music, wrote them on a scrap of paper at Julia Mitchell's house, and left the music there. When he returned months later from a business trip to New York, Julia reminded him to finish the song, which she thought was promising. As she entered the living room later that evening, Stephen sat at the piano, playing the song again and again. With "Old Dog Tray," Stephen had progressed from writing Ethiopian songs to plantation melodies to American melodies.

Old Dog Tray

The morn of life is past,
And evening comes at last;
It brings me a dream of a once happy day,
Of merry forms I've seen
Upon the village green,
Sporting with my old dog Tray.

Chorus

Old dog Tray's ever faithful,
Grief cannot drive him away.
He's gentle, he is kind;
I'll never, never find
A better friend than old dog Tray.

On January 16, 1857, Stephen wrote a letter to Billy Hamilton regarding a different dog:

Dear Billy,

I am much obliged to you for that dog, "Rat-trap" as we called him, on account of his well known ferocity towards those animals. You must pardon me if I inform you that he is now with us no more. He continued to devour shoes, stockings, spools, the cat, and every thing else that he could find lying around loose. At last we held a council of war, and thought we would put him in the yard, then we thought we wouldn't. We concluded at last to put him in the cellar. There he stayed for three days and howled all the time, and would have howled till now if I had not let him out. I was afraid the neighbors would inform on us for keeping a nuisance. Solitary confinement did not agree with him. He lost his appetite. Then I gave him some garlic as you had instructed me. This gave him a sort of diarrhea, and he got into Mit's room and relieved himself on his bed, then he scattered his dirty shirts over the floor, sprinkled his shoes and played hob generally. This performance seemed to bring him to his appetite, for that same evening he stole a whole beef steak off the kitchen table and swallowed it all raw. We concluded this was too much to stand even from "Friendships offering", so I made up my mind to trade him off. John Little had a friend in Chicago who wanted just such a dog, so he gave me a very fine Scotch terrier Eighteen months old for him. "Trap" is enjoying the lake breezes.

Your friend,
S.C. Foster

Blackie, the Scotch terrier received in the trade, scampered alongside Stephen and his daughter, Marion, on their jaunt to the park each day. Marion romped with the dog while Stephen rested on the park lawn and enjoyed the summer air, the warbling of birds, and the muted blasts of the steamboat whistles from the river some distance away. The threesome proceeded to the canal where Stephen chatted with the toll taker every day for a month before the man learned he was talking with Stephen Foster, the well-known songwriter.

The Fosters loved Blackie, their cherished pet. "Old Dog Tray" was published in 1853, several years before Rat-trap and Blackie turned up. And Tray, a beautiful setter, though a good friend to Stephen, belonged to Matthew Stewart, a neighbor who lived on the West Common.

Title page of sheet music, "Jeanie with the Light Brown Hair." Courtesy of the Foster Hall Collection, Center for American Music, University of Pittsburgh Library System

Chapter Nine

Jeanie with the Light Brown Hair

Jane left Stephen in the spring of 1853 and took little Marion with her to Lewistown, Pennsylvania, to live with her widowed mother. Stephen had divided his attention among his parents, his wife, and his songwriting. Jane may have felt deprived of her share of his devotion, or Jane's conservative and practical personality collided with Stephen's artistic and impulsive nature.

After Jane left, Stephen moved to New York as a celebrity. His well-known songs made him a popular composer, though some columnists disapproved of the minstrel tunes. In June of 1853, Stephen wrote to Mit saying he had plenty of work to keep him busy.

Stephen's *The Social Orchestra*,* published the following January, included his own songs and arrangements of other composers' works in solo, duet, trio and quartet forms for piano, flute, and violin. He included waltzes, quadrilles, polkas, schottisches, and quicksteps all popular dance steps of the day. Because dance halls were off-limits to young people of prominent families, teens made their own music at home and danced in their own living rooms. The parlor and its piano stood at the center of family entertainment. As a result, Stephen's *Social Orchestra* sold well.

Stephen lived in the dreams of his songs or in the clouds of melancholy, but in spite of his passion for music and poetry, he missed his wife and daughter when they lived apart from him. Stephen wrote "Jeanie with the Light Brown Hair" for Jane, perhaps to woo her home.

Jeanie with the Light Brown Hair

I dream of Jeanie with the light brown hair,
Borne, like a vapor, on the summer air
I see her tripping where the bright streams play,
Happy as the daisies that dance on the way.

Many were the wild notes her merry voice would pour,
Many were the blithe birds that warbled them o'er:
Oh! I dream of Jeanie with the light brown hair,
Floating like a vapor on the soft summer air.

Marion said her mother confided that Stephen fell in love first with
Jane's hair. Stephen originally wrote the song as "Jennie with the Light
Brown Hair." He changed "Jennie," as Jane was affectionately called, to
Jeanie when a publisher pointed out how many times Foster had used the
name "Jennie" in other songs, including "Jenny's Coming O'er the Green"
and "Jennie's Own Schottische."

During the winter of 1853 or the spring of 1854, Jane and Marion
reunited with Stephen. First, they occupied a boarding house in Manhattan
and later moved to a brownstone in Hoboken. "Jeanie with the Light Brown
Hair" was published in the summer of 1854.

By fall of 1854, they were all back in Allegheny, living with Stephen's
parents. William B. Foster Sr. no longer recognized his family members.
When a housekeeper left, the brothers pooled their money and hired another
to help care for their father.

Dunning, in failing health, improved enough to make a trip home by
Christmas, so the Christmas of 1854 found all the sons except Brother
William at home with their mother and father. Brother William lived with
his family in Philadelphia and worked as vice president of the Pennsylvania
Railroad.

The Foster children anticipated the death of their bedridden father, but to
their shock and grief, Eliza died first while on a shopping trip to Pittsburgh
in January of 1855. She had ridden to town in a hired carriage, purchased
a measure of blue ribbon, and felt sudden pain as she walked along the
street. Eliza collapsed on a sofa in a nearby house where she knew the
residents, but when the physician from next door arrived, she had passed
away. She was buried in the cemetery near Lawrenceville, the town
William Sr. had mapped out many years before, less than a mile from
their beloved White Cottage. Eliza lay next to Charlotte, whose remains
had been moved from Louisville to Allegheny in 1852. Six months
later, when William Sr. died, another funeral took place and another burial
in the family plot.

Dunning summoned his brothers to Cincinnati during March of the following year; and with Stephen, Henry, and Mit by his side, Dunning died from the tuberculosis, which had plagued him since the Mexican War. The brothers sailed with Dunning on his last steamboat ride, home to Pittsburgh. Except for a stint as a soldier, he had spent his adult life on the river: from clerk to merchant, to steamboat captain, to steamboat owner. He never married but had many friends up and down the rivers.

Brother William couldn't be in Pittsburgh to see the riverboat flags waving at half-mast for Dunning. He had moved Elizabeth to a southern climate for her respiratory condition. But before the end of 1856, Elizabeth lay in the family cemetery near Lawrenceville, beside the baby girl they had lost several years before.

It's no wonder that Stephen sometimes wrote songs about death and dedicated songs to dead friends. In the nineteenth century, death and grief intruded, with grim reality, into everyday life.

After Dunning's death, Ann Eliza wrote in a letter to Mit:

> *With a great deal of love to Henry and Stephen,—say to them, as soldiers in battle close together as death thins their ranks, so I trust shall we become more firmly united in heart as our number decreases. I shall hope to hear from them before long and from you, too, dear Mitty, as soon as possible.*
>
> *Your attached Sister,*
> *Ann Eliza*

The surviving siblings continued to love and care for one another. Fortunately for the Fosters, outside forces intervened to distract them from their grief. Stephen and Mit immersed themselves in a national presidential campaign.

Chapter Ten

The White House Chair

Ann Eliza (Foster) Buchanan's brother-in-law ran for president of the United States in 1856. James Buchanan, the Democrat, ran against John C. Fremont, the Republican, and Millard Fillmore, the Whig*. (The Republican Party was formed in 1854 and held its first convention in Pittsburgh in 1856.) The Democrats managed their campaign without making an issue of slavery. They wanted to keep the union intact and avoid war. The Republican's antislavery campaign slogan was "Freedom, Free Men, Fremont." The Whigs* played one side against the other.

Stephen served as musical director of the James Buchanan Glee Club and wrote songs for the group. He, Mit, and Billy Hamilton were charter members of this political marching and singing band. The following campaign song, written by Stephen, is a call for national unity:

The White House Chair

Let all our hearts for union be,
For the North and South are one;
They've worked together manfully
And together they will still work on.

Chorus

Then come ye men from every state,
Our creed is broad and fair;
Buchanan is our candidate,
And we'll put him in the White House Chair.

During marches and choral performances with the Buchanan Glee Club, Stephen and the other singers walked with a bodyguard. The guards were silent during the main part of the song and chimed in for the chorus. During one performance, Billy heard a member of the audience singing off-key. He alerted a guard to ask the man to sing only the chorus with the guards. The guard misunderstood and tried to expel the out-of-tune offender. A fight broke out, and when the firemen from across the street joined the brawl, Stephen and his friends—mostly smaller guys and unwilling fighters—ran for safety.

Ordinarily not involved in politics, Stephen felt enthusiasm for Buchanan's candidacy, partly due to family loyalties and partly as a new outlet for his creative impulses. The singing, parading, and campaigning paid off when James Buchanan was inaugurated as president in March of 1857.

As Democrats, the Fosters didn't oppose slavery, and they had used indentured servants* to help with housekeeping, but the McDowells were against slavery. Jane's father, Dr. McDowell, helped Martin Delaney enter Harvard Medical School as its first black American student. Delaney— writer, soldier, and abolitionist—divided his time between fighting slavery and practicing medicine. He served as a surgeon during the civil war and became the first black man to achieve the rank of major. Charles Shiras— Stephen's best friend until he died in 1854—also a staunch abolitionist, briefly edited an abolitionist publication, the *Albatross*. Surrounded by these influences, Stephen developed a social consciousness that compelled him to write his folk songs with sensitivity, lending dignity to blacks.

In 1858, Stephen, Jane, and Marion made a round-trip pleasure trip from Pittsburgh to Cincinnati on the steamboat *Ida May* where Stephen's friend Billy Hamilton—the donor of the wicked dog, "Rat-trap"—worked as a clerk.

One evening, Billy and Stephen walked down Broadway in a Cincinnati residential area on the way back to their steamboat. They heard a group singing in a nearby garden and recognized the strains of "Come Where My Love Lies Dreaming." Billy thought the singers were "bungling" the song. Stephen and Billy crossed the street and joined the serenade uninvited. When their intrusion annoyed the choristers, Billy introduced Stephen as the composer of the melody they had been singing. They didn't believe it;

so Billy and Stephen took the group to Cons Miller—the river editor of the *Commercial Gazette*, whom all parties knew and trusted—to vouch for Stephen. After the group was convinced of Stephen's identity, they treated the pair like royalty.

"Nothing was too good for us," Billy reported.

Chapter Eleven

Old Black Joe

Stephen's income from his songwriting fell short of what he needed. During his most productive years, between 1849 and 1860, he earned an average of one thousand three hundred seventy dollars per year, enough to support one person at that time but not enough to pay the expenses for a family of three. Sometimes he got behind in paying the rent on William's house, and often, he borrowed ahead from his publishers. In the first years following the deaths of his parents, he published fewer songs. Stephen kept a studio in the middle of Bohemian Pittsburgh, surrounded by music stores filled with musicians and entertainers, including minstrels. But most of his musical creations were "parlor music," which earned him little. To square his debts, he gave up rights to sixteen of his earlier popular songs by selling off future royalties to his publishers, Firth, Pond & Co.

Stephen was lonely in Pittsburgh. His best friend and one of the "Knights," Charles Shiras, had died in 1854, and in 1855, his beloved parents died. He lost his brother Dunning in 1856. When Brother William sold his house in Allegheny in the spring of 1857, Stephen and family moved to the Eagle Hotel on Liberty Street where Stephen stayed alone when Jane and little Marion, sometimes, visited Jane's sisters out of town.

In February of 1858, Mit spent time in Philadelphia, helping Brother William who had suffered from loneliness and health problems since Elizabeth's death. In February of 1860, Mit married Jesse Lightner, an old friend of the "Knights" and a singer of Foster songs. They moved to Cleveland where Mit took a job as assistant director of the Juniata Iron Works.

Brother William couldn't come to Jesse and Mit's wedding due to a troublesome abscess on his neck. The abscess finally healed but from the outside only, and on March 4, 1860, their faithful Brother William died from a brain infection. Once again, flags flew at half-mast, this time at the train stations between Philadelphia and Pittsburgh. A railcar covered in a black drape brought Brother William home. Another Foster burial took place in the Allegheny cemetery.

Henry and family were the only Fosters left in Pittsburgh when Stephen, Jane, and Marion departed for New York by way of Warren, Ohio, in the spring of 1860. Henrietta and her family had moved to Warren from Youngstown. Stephen's family divided their time in Warren between Henrietta's home and a local hotel, the Gaskill House.

During their four-month stay in Warren, Stephen spent some of his time composing. He wrote to Mit, asking for a temporary loan of twelve dollars.

"I have written two songs since I have been in Warren and have two under way but do not feel inclined to send them off half made up."

Though he didn't have a big voice, he had a fine baritone range and enjoyed singing and entertaining on spontaneous occasions. He sang and played piano in the large public parlor of the Gaskill House. Marion played dolls with the proprietor's daughter in the empty ballroom. The girls danced, and Marion played castanets while Stephen stood in the door and watched and applauded.

Stephen wore a high silk hat during his time in Warren, with which he waved goodbye to the proprietor's family as he, Jane, and Marion boarded the stagecoach for their trip to New York.

After the Foster family arrived in New York in the fall of 1860, they settled into the boarding house of Mrs. Louisa Stewart on Greene Street. Mrs. Stewart's daughters enjoyed having little Marion with them, and a friendship formed between the Fosters and the Stewarts.

During the years since Stephen's parents' deaths, he hadn't published many songs, and his celebrity status had diminished since his first move to New York in 1853. In 1860, Stephen recovered his muse* and sent several songs to the publishers, including "The Glendy Burk," a river song, and "Old Black Joe," a song about a servant anticipating death.

Stephen Foster no longer wrote for Christy, who had died, and "Old Black Joe," written in the fall of 1860, contained no dialect. Stephen wrote the song for Joe, who had been the butler at Jane (McDowell) Foster's home in the days when the young men had come to call on the six daughters. Joe joked and kidded with the boys as he put their gifts of flowers in vases and took their coats and hats. Stephen especially liked him, telling him, "Joe, I'm going to put you in a song one day."

Old Black Joe

Gone are the days
When my heart was young and gay*,
Gone are my friends
From the cotton fields away,
Gone from the earth
To a better land I know
I hear their gentle voices calling
"Old Black Joe."

Chorus

I'm coming, I'm coming,
For my head is bending low:
I hear those gentle voices calling
"Old Black Joe."

Old Joe was "gone from the earth" when Stephen finally wrote the song. Jane Foster would not allow it sung in her presence. Whatever memories the tune evoked for Jane, she couldn't hear "Old Black Joe" without breaking into tears.

Title page of sheet music, "The Glendy Burk." Courtesy of the Foster Hall Collection, Center for American Music, University of Pittsburgh Library System

Part Four

New York

1860-1864

Chapter Twelve

Dear Friends and Gentle Hearts

The climate in the country was tumultuous as tensions between the North and the South reached the breaking point. With the election of Abraham Lincoln to the presidency in 1860, the southern states began to secede, one by one. And when the Confederates fired on Fort Sumter in April of 1861, the civil war erupted despite all efforts to avoid it.

At some point in 1861, Jane and Marion left New York and returned to Lewistown, Pennsylvania, where Jane's mother and sister lived, and Stephen was on his own for the remainder of his life. Marion would have been about ten years old, Jane thirty-two, and Stephen thirty-five.

Mustering soldiers became a difficult task in New York where half the population were foreign-born and indifferent to the conflicts dividing the country. Riots erupted in the streets when protesters torched two draft offices, one of them in Stephen's neighborhood. Stephen was exempted from the draft, but many young men had to serve. A rich man could hire himself a substitute or pay three hundred dollars to be excused from serving in the Union Army, but a poor man had to enlist or be drafted. Enthusiasm had turned to despair among the soldiers by the second winter of hunger, disease, and cold. Deserters fled both armies.

The American songwriter struggled to survive in a climate at odds with his nature, in an atmosphere lacking optimism and security. The country paid its highest toll ever for freedom's cause with the decimation of the nation's young male population. Stephen turned to rum for solace. Gradually, he gave in to its power.

"It was the only failing he ever had," said Mit. (William Sr. had fought the same enemy during Stephen's youth.) Stephen took cures and had spells of sobriety during the New York years. A nephew, sent to see about him and to try to bring him home, found him completely sober.

Stephen wrote soldier songs and hymns but barely earned enough for food and lodging. The copyright laws were not honored in the South during the war, so he didn't receive royalties for sheet music sold south of the Mason-Dixon Line where his music had gained the most popularity. He often cranked out ordinary compositions during the war years, not always the music of his genius.

George Cooper and John Mahon became his friends in New York. Cooper, fourteen years younger, studied law while soldiering for the Union Army. During army furloughs,Cooper indulged his interest in poetry. He became Stephen's protégé and wrote the words to many of his songs. Stephen called Cooper "the left wing of the song factory."[1] The publisher, John J. Daley bought many of their collaborations for cash instead of royalties.

Cooper reported that Stephen composed the music for one of Cooper's poems on an upside-down cheese crate in a barroom. After looking over the poem, Stephen took a piece of music paper from his pocket, put it on the crate, and smoothed out the creases. Ignoring the socializing going on around him, and running his fingers up and down the imaginary piano keys on top of the crate, he quickly contrived the melody and then the piano accompaniment.

"Now for a publisher," he said as he finished the song and scooped up some sand from the floor to sprinkle on the paper to help dry the ink.

John Mahon, eleven years older than Stephen, worked as a newspaper reporter. He and his wife and daughters welcomed Stephen into their home. Though Stephen wrote many songs at their piano, he and Mahon collaborated on only one piece. Stephen Foster arranged, for the piano, "Our Darling Kate," with words and music by John Mahon, a tribute to an actress friend of Mahon's.

Once, when both were penniless, Stephen sat at Mahon's piano and revived a song that Pond, the publisher, had rejected. It took him about an hour and a half to rewrite from memory the words and music to "Our Bright, Bright Summer Days Are Gone." Mahon took it to John J. Daley, a different publisher, who was happy to get a Foster song and paid a good sum for it, "though not a tithe of what Foster got in his better days," wrote Mahon.

Stephen remembered all of his own music but forgot the words to all of his songs except "Hard Times." Mahon took Stephen to a Temperance* meeting in New York where Stephen entertained the crowd with "Hard Times, Come Again No More." Stephen sang with such feeling that tears came to the eyes of many of the listeners.

Stephen's war songs defend the Union but do not mention slavery. The following is a verse of the bold and lively "That's What's the Matter." Stephen Foster wrote the words and the music:

That's What's the Matter

We live in hard and stirring times,
Too sad for mirth, too rough for rhymes,
For songs of peace have lost their chimes,
And that's what's the matter.
The men we held as brothers true
Have turned into a rebel crew,
So we have to put them through,
And that's what's the matter.

Chorus

That's what's the matter,
The rebels have to scatter;
We'll make them flee by land and sea,
And that's what's the matter!

Stephen's sister Henrietta, his brother Mit, and Mit's wife, Jesse, did not approve of the pro-Union lyrics present in many of Stephen's soldier songs, some of which he wrote with George Cooper.

Many of the Foster-Cooper collaborations were musically appealing, including their comical songs. One called "If You've Only Got a Moustache" asserts that a guy will have all the girlfriends he wants if he will simply grow a moustache. Two other examples of their witty compositions are "Mr. and Mrs. Brown" and "There Are Plenty of Fish in the Sea." A few years later, Gilbert and Sullivan, the British songwriting team, would compose pieces reminiscent of the Foster-Cooper ones for the British light opera stage: spirited tunes with humorous rhymes.

Stephen loved riding the crowded horse-drawn omnibuses through New York. The clip-clop of the horses' hooves jostled his musical muse*. Occasionally, he would pen the lines of a music staff on his thumbnail and write a few notes there in order to keep a tune alive until he had access to paper. According to Mahon, Stephen said,

> "There is so much music running through my brain that I will miss it unless I put a note or two down to jog my memory."

In 1863, the composer created more songs than ever—fifty of them—almost one-fourth of his total lifetime output. Half of them were hymns.

Jane learned to operate the telegraph machine and worked as a telegrapher over the next several years. She supported her child in that way and assisted Mrs. McDowell and Jane's sister Agnes in the finances of their Lewistown household. During the civil war, Jane worked at the Pennsylvania Railroad Station in Greensburg, which is 33 miles east of Pittsburgh and 135 miles west of Lewistown. She handled important telegrams: war notices, troop-movement advisories, messages of death, and of safety and survival.

Though they lived apart, Jane was Stephen's best advocate during his last years. Her concern for his welfare is evident in her correspondence with Mit on Stephen's behalf and her periodic visits to New York to see about him. Jane schemed—unsuccessfully—with Mit to persuade Stephen to come to Cleveland and live with Mit's family.

John Mahon and George Cooper were disturbed by the decline in Stephen's health and his poor diet, but the composer rebuffed their suggestions or interferences. Food was not important to Stephen, and sometimes his meal consisted of raw turnips or an apple, which he peeled with a large pocketknife. His shabby clothing bothered Mit, but when Stephen received new clothes, he sold them and wore the old ones—again. Mit once said,

"Why are you so careless, Steve? If I went around like that, I'd be afraid of being insulted." Stephen replied,

> "Don't worry about me, Mitty. No gentleman will insult me— and no other can!"

One morning, weakened from fever after being ill for several days, he rose from bed to get a drink of water and fell against the washbowl, cutting a gash in his face and neck and badly bruising his forehead. The chambermaid found him in a pool of blood and summoned George Cooper to Stephen's boarding house at no. 15 Bowery, known then as the North American Hotel.

Stephen looked up at George with his wonderful brown eyes and said, "I'm done for."

In addition to the new wounds, he had a nasty burn on his thigh—medically untreated—from a recent accident with an overturned oil lamp.

George figured the doctor who sewed Stephen's wound, since he stitched him up with black thread instead of white, was no good. Actually, the color of the suture material probably didn't matter. But together, George and the doctor got Stephen dressed and accompanied him to Bellevue Hospital where he died three days later on Wednesday, January 13, 1864, while the civil war still raged on. George sent a telegram to Mit who came to New York with Jane and Henry to claim Stephen's body and to take him home to Pittsburgh.

At the hospital, the family received his personal things in a small sack: Stephen's clothes, his worn leather money purse containing thirty-eight cents—all the money he had in the world—and a tattered scrap of brown paper penciled by his own hand, perhaps the first line of an intended song, "Dear friends and gentle hearts."

When they arrived at Winterbottom, the undertaker on Broome Street, Jane fell to the floor in grief next to Stephen's casket and remained there for some time.

Stephen's body and his family members traveled on separate trains of the Pennsylvania Railroad, home to Pittsburgh, free of charge.

Stephen's old friend Henry Kleber arranged the music for the funeral in the Trinity Episcopal Church, the same church of his baptism and marriage. As friends lowered Stephen into his grave in the family cemetery, a band of musicians played "Come Where My Love Lies Dreaming" and "Old Folks at Home." Mit wrote in his short biography of Stephen,

"His body lies beside the mother and father he loved so much and near the spot where he was born."

Scrap of paper found in Stephen's pocket upon his death, "Dear friends and gentle hearts," perhaps the title for another song. Courtesy of the Foster Hall Collection, Center for American Music, University of Pittsburgh Library System

Stephen (left) with his friend George Cooper, Courtesy of the Foster Hall Collection, Center for American Music, University of Pittsburgh Library System

Title page of sheet music, "Beautiful Dreamer." Courtesy of the Foster Hall Collection, Center for American Music, University of Pittsburgh Library System

Chapter Thirteen

Beautiful Dreamer

After the civil war, Congress made a law establishing the Library of Congress as the only body to issue copyrights, simplifying the copyright confusion of Stephen's world. Today, the works of composers are protected through the American Society of Composers, Authors and Publishers founded in 1914. Composers earn anytime their pieces are used for public performance: on the radio, on television, or on the soundtracks of movies. Laws to protect artists didn't exist in Stephen's time. The publishers ruled. Stephen would have attained enormous wealth had he been fairly paid. Instead, he worried daily about subsistence. Remarkably, regardless of hardships, his creative spirit survived.

Driven by an unrelenting combination of destiny and determination, Stephen Foster pioneered American songwriting. He crafted his music as bravely as the frontiersmen slashed their trails. The values expressed in the songs relate to a universal need to connect, to belong, to have a home, friends, and family. Foster's nostalgia for a lost home was especially meaningful to the people of a nation influx, for people moving off of the farms and into the cities and migrating from the Atlantic to the Pacific. Stephen connected with his countrymen in a way no American musician had done before.

The fun in the comic songs, the melancholy in the spirituals, and the friendship in the ballads were the poetry and melody of Stephen's heart. In the light of his path, future musicians and songwriters would forge a more profitable course, and upon the cornerstones of his foundation would the popular musical culture of the nation be established.

In addition to the memorials in White Springs, Florida, and Bardstown, Kentucky, a complete collection of Stephen's music and memorabilia is contained in the Foster Hall Collection at the Center for American Music, University of Pittsburgh. The collections of Josiah K. Lilly, a philanthropist and Foster enthusiast, are housed there. A permanent staff preserves the sheet music and historical records and catalogue articles relative to Stephen C. Foster. This fine museum is located in the Stephen Foster Memorial, a building erected in Foster's memory. A statue of Foster with Old Uncle Ned (one of his song characters) stands across the street, in the park, next to the Carnegie Museum. Hundreds of people visit Stephen's gravesite each year, and there are monuments to him all over the country.

Stephen was the first musician elected to the Hall of Fame for Great Americans. On the campus of the Bronx Community College of the City University of New York, the bust of Stephen Foster takes its place in the grand colonnade in the company of Thomas Edison, Mark Twain, Nathaniel Hawthorne, Washington Irving, Orville and Wilbur Wright, George Washington, Benjamin Franklin, George Washington Carver, John Philip Sousa, Edgar Allen Poe, and other great Americans.

Though the publishers had the music available, "Beautiful Dreamer," written in 1862, wasn't published until after Stephen's death. Stephen wrote the words and the music. His brilliance is stunningly restored in this weaving of music with mermaids, moonlight, and mist. This song of dreams is an expression of hope that the clouds of sorrow will lift when the dreamer awakens. It's the song Lewis sings to Serena to awaken her in E. B. White's children's book *The Trumpet of the Swan*. And it's Stephen's swan song*, his last great composition.

Beautiful Dreamer

Beautiful dreamer, wake unto me,
Starlight and dewdrops are waiting for thee;
Sounds of the rude world heard in the day,
Lull'd by the moonlight have all pass'd away!
Beautiful dreamer, queen of my song,
List while I woo thee with soft melody;
Gone are the cares of life's busy throng,
Beautiful dreamer, awake unto me!
Beautiful dreamer, awake unto me!

Beautiful dreamer, out on the sea
Mermaids are chanting the wild lorelie;
Over the streamlet vapors are borne,
Waiting to fade at the bright coming morn.
Beautiful dreamer, beam on my heart,
E'en as the morn on the streamlet and sea;
Then will all clouds of sorrow depart,
Beautiful dreamer, awake unto me!
Beautiful dreamer, awake unto me!

Acknowledgments

This is my first book, and I want to express my gratitude to the following friends and family members who read the first draft, offered suggestions, and gave encouragement: Phyllis Hunter, Craig Hunter, Ward Hunter, Gini Hunter, Anne Webster, Karen Albert, Eric Ulken, and Jerry Watts, MD.

Thank you all, my editors, professional and nonprofessional, for your advice, even when I didn't take it: Eric Ulken, Jerry Watts, Craig Hunter, Anne Webster, Denise Sutherland, James Nolan and the editors at Xlibris. I'm grateful to the participants of various writers' workshops, notably Charlotte Parker, Ron Dill, and Anna Marie Catoir for their suggestions. Thanks are due to Maria Baisier, who gave the manuscript to three of her junior-high students to read and critique. "Not enough action and adventure," one said.

Special thanks go to my friend Jerry Watts, who traveled with me to all three of the Stephen Foster memorials, twice each; and to my son, Eric, a journalist, who taught me to use the computer for word processing, and rescued me when I got stuck. Without Jerry and Eric, this little book would not exist.

I'm grateful to Kathryn M. Haines at the Stephen Foster Memorial and Museum, Center for American Music, University of Pittsburgh. She corrected historical errors in the first drafts, offered useful suggestions for content, gave encouragement all along the way, and assisted with providing the images for the book. I want to express my appreciation to her assistant, Nathan Bowers, who showed us the Foster sheet-music collection and other treasures on our first visit to the museum.

I appreciate the cooperation of Arlene Railey, Courtney Livengood, and Valinda Subic at the Stephen Foster Folk Culture Center in White Springs, Florida, in making possible the use of the Christy painting for the book cover. A special thanks goes to Priscilla and Lance Strozier for providing a copy of Priscilla's photograph of the painting to be used on the cover.

Chronology

July 4, 1826—Stephen Collins Foster is born in Lawrenceville, Pennsylvania (Pittsburgh).

1829—The family moves from the White Cottage and is transient for the next several years.

1833—When Stephen is seven years old, he plays a song on a flute in a music store in Pittsburgh when he had never played such a flute before.

1835—At age nine, Stephen is the "star" of an amateur minstrel show made up of the neighborhood children.

1840—Brother William takes Stephen to Towanda for schooling and takes over the responsibility of his education.

Spring 1841—Stephen, aged fourteen, composes *Tioga Waltz* for a school function in Athens, Pennsylvania (published after Stephen's death by Mit and from Mit's memory).

Summer 1841—At fifteen years of age, Stephen quits Jefferson College and moves home to Pittsburgh.

December 1844—He publishes his first song, "Open Thy Lattice Love."

Late in 1846 or early 1847—Stephen moves to Cincinnati to work for Dunning.

1847—"Oh! Susanna" is written, the success of which led Stephen to follow songwriting as a career. The first published edition (without Stephen's name) was issued in February1848 by the publisher Holt. The authorized edition by the publisher Peters was issued in December 1848.

Summer 1849—Stephen contracts a recurring febrile* illness during his last summer in Cincinnati. "Nelly Was a Lady" is published.

1850—Stephen moves home to Pittsburgh and marries Jane Denny McDowell. "Nelly Bly" and "Camptown Races" are published.

1851—Marion, the only child of Jane and Stephen, is born in Pittsburgh. "Old Folks at Home" is published.

February 20, 1852—Jane and Stephen and several friends make a river cruise to New Orleans.

1852—"My Old Kentucky Home" is written (published in 1853).

December 11, 1852—The railroad reaches Pittsburgh. The trip to New York now takes less than a day as opposed to four days overland prior to the railroad.

1853—Jane and Stephen separate. Stephen moves to New York and publishes *The Social Orchestra*. "Jeanie with the Light Brown Hair" is written (published in 1854).

Winter 1853 or spring 1854—Stephen and Jane reunite in Manhattan. By fall, they are back in Allegheny with the Foster family.

1855—Stephen's parents die, Eliza first in January and William Sr. six months later. "Come Where My Love Lies Dreaming" is published.

1856—Dunning dies. "Gentle Annie" is published.

1860—Brother William dies. Jane, Stephen, and Marion move to New York. "Old Black Joe" and "The Glendy Burk" are published.

1861—Jane and Marion move to Lewistown, leaving Stephen alone in New York. "Our Bright, Bright Summer days are Gone" is published. The civil war begins in April.

1862—"Beautiful Dreamer" is written.

1863—Stephen publishes fifty songs, one quarter of his lifetime output.

January 13, 1864—Stephen dies in New York City in Bellevue Hospital. "Beautiful Dreamer" is published after his death.

Title page of "Home Songster." Courtesy of the Foster Hall Collection,
Center for American Music, University of Pittsburgh Library System

Chronological List of Songs Compositions and Arrangements

1844
Open Thy Lattice Love

1846
There's a Good Time Coming

1847
Lou'siana Belle
What Must a Fairy's Dream Be?

1848
Away Down South
Oh! Susanna
Old Uncle Ned
Santa Anna's Retreat from Buena Vista
Stay Summer Breath

1849
Dolcy Jones
My Brudder Gum
Nelly Was a Lady
Summer Longings

1850
Ah! May the Red Rose Live Always
Angelina Baker
Camptown Races
Dolly Day
I Would Not Die in Spring Time

Lily Ray
Mary Loves the Flowers
Molly Do you Love Me?
Nelly Bly
Oh! Lemuel!
Soiree Polka
The Spirit of My Song
Turn Not Away!
Village Bells Polka
The Voice of Bygone Days
Way Down in Ca-i-ro

1851

Eulalie
Farewell my Lilly Dear
Farewell! Old Cottage
Give the Stranger Happy Cheer
I Would Not Die in Summer Time
In the Eye Abides the Heart
Laura Lee
Melinda May
Mother, Thou'rt Faithful to Me
My Hopes Have Departed Forever
Oh! Boys, Carry Me 'Long
Old Folks at Home
Once I Loved Thee Mary Dear
Ring the Banjo
Sweetly She Sleeps, My Alice Fair
Willie My Brave
Wilt Thou Be Gone, Love?

1852

Camptown Races (song with guitar accompaniment)
The Hour for Thee and Me
I Cannot Sing To-Night
Laura Lee (song with guitar accompaniment)
Maggie by My Side
Massa's in the Cold Ground

1853

Annie My Own Love
Eulalie (song with guitar accompaniment)
Farewell My Lilly Dear (song with guitar accompaniment)
The Holiday Schottische
Little Ella
Massa's in the Cold Ground (song with guitar accompaniment)
Massa's in the Cold Ground (Foster's melodies arranged for the guitar)
My Old Kentucky Home, Good-Night
My Old Kentucky Home, Good-Night (song with guitar accompaniment)
Oh! Boys, Carry Me 'Long (song with guitar accompaniment)
Oh! Boys, Carry Me 'Long (Foster's melodies arranged for the guitar)
Old Dog Tray
Old Folks Quadrilles
Old Memories
There's a Land of Bliss
Willie My Brave (song with guitar accompaniment)

1854

Come with Thy Sweet Voice Again
Come with Thy Sweet Voice Again (Foster's melodies arranged for the guitar)
Ellen Bayne
Ellen Bayne (Foster's melodies arranged for the guitar)
Jeanie with the Light Brown Hair
Jeanie with the Light Brown Hair (Foster's melodies arranged for the guitar)
Little Ella (Foster's melodies arranged for the guitar)
Maggie by My Side (Foster's melodies arranged for the guitar)
Old Dog Tray (Foster's melodies arranged for the guitar)
Old Memories (Foster's melodies arranged for the guitar)
The Social Orchestra
Willie We Have Missed You
Willie We Have Missed You (Foster's melodies arranged for the guitar)

1855

Come Where My Love Lies Dreaming
Comrades, Fill No Glass for Me
Hard Times Come Again No More
Hard Times Come Again No More (song with guitar accompaniment)

84

Some Folks
The Village Maiden

1856
Gentle Annie
The Great Baby Show or The Abolition Show

1857
Gentle Annie (song with guitar accompaniment)
I See Her Still in My Dreams

1858
Linger in Blissful Repose
Lula Is Gone
My Loved One and My Own or Eva
Sadly to Mine Heart Appealing
Some Folks (song with guitar accompaniment)
Where Has Lula Gone?

1859
Fairy-Belle
For Thee, Love, for Thee
Linda Has Departed
Parthenia to Ingomar
Sorrow Shall Come Again No More
Thou Art the Queen of My Song

1860
Beautiful Child of Song
Cora Dean
Down among the Cane-Brakes
The Glendy Burk
Jenny's Coming O'er the Green
The Little Ballad Girl
None Shall Weep a Tear for Me
Old Black Joe
Poor Drooping Maiden
Under the Willow She's Sleeping

Virginia Belle
The Wife or He'll Come Home

1861

Don't Bet Your Money on de Shanghai
Farewell Mother Dear
Farewell Sweet Mother
I'll Be a Soldier
Little Belle Blair
Lizzie Dies Tonight
Mine Is the Mourning Heart
Molly Dear Good Night
Nell and I
Oh! Tell Me of My Mother
Our Bright, Bright Summer Days Are Gone
Our Willie Dear Is Dying
A Penny for Your Thoughts
Sweet Little Maid of the Mountain
Why Have My Loved Ones Gone?

1862

Better Times Are Coming
A Dream of My Mother and My Home
Gentle Lena Clare
Happy Hours at Home
I'll Be Home To-Morrow
I Will Be True to Thee
Little Jenny Dow
Merry Little Birds Are We
The Merry, Merry Month of May
No Home, No Home
Slumber My Darling
That's What's the Matter
There Are Plenty of Fish in the Sea
Was My Brother in the Battle?
We Are Coming Father Abraam, 300,000 More
We've a Million in the Field
Why No One to Love?

1863

The Angels Are Singing unto Me
The Beautiful Shore
The Bright Hills of Glory
Bring My Brother Back to Me
Bury Me in the Morning, Mother
Choral Harp
Don't Be Idle
For the Dear Old Flag I Die!
Give Us This Day Our Daily Bread
Happy Little Ones Are We
He Leadeth Me beside Still Waters
Home, Heavenly Home!
I'd Be a Fairy
Jenny June
Katy Bell
Kissing in the Dark
Larry's Goodbye
Leave Me with My Mother
Lena Our Loved One Is Gone
Little Ella's an Angel!
The Love I Bear to Thee
Music Everywhere, That's Why I Love It So
My Boy Is Coming from the War
My Wife Is a Most Knowing Woman
Nothing but a Plain Old Soldier
Oh! 'Tis Glorious
Oh! There's No Such Girl As Mine
Oh! Why Am I So Happy?
Onward and Upward!
Over the River
The Pure, the Bright, the Beautiful
Seek and Ye Shall Find
A Soldier in the Colored Brigade
The Soldier's Home
The Song of All Songs
Stand Up for the Truth

Suffer Little Children to Come unto Me
Tears Bring Thoughts of Heaven
Tell Me of the Angels, Mother
There Is a Land of Love
There Was a Time
We'll All Meet Our Saviour
We Will Keep a Bright Lookout
We'll Still Keep Marching On
We'll Tune Our Hearts
What Shall the Harvest Be?
When This Dreadful War Is Ended
While We Work for the Lord
Willie's Gone to Heaven
Willie Has Gone to the War

1864

All Day Long
Beautiful Dreamer
Give This to Mother
Golden Dreams and Fairy Castles!
If You've Only Got a Moustache
Little Mac! Little Mac! You're the Very Man
Mr. and Mrs. Brown
She Was All the World to Me
Sitting by My Own Cabin Door
Somebody's Coming to See Me Tonight
Tell Me Love of Thy Early Dreams
When Dear Friends Are Gone
When Old Friends Were Here
Wilt Thou Be True

1865

My Angel Boy, I Cannot See Thee Die
Oh! Meet Me Dear Mother
Our Darling Kate
Stand Up for the Flag
The Voices That Are Gone

1866
Sweet Emerald Isle That I Love So Well

1867
Praise the Lord

1869
Dearer Than Life!
Kiss Me Dear Mother Ere I Die

1870
A Thousand Miles from Home
While the Bowl Goes Round

1885
The White House Chair

1895
Where Is Thy Spirit Mary?

1896
The Tioga Waltz

1931
Long Ago Day
This Rose Will Remind You

Glossary

blackface—An actor's face blackened with burnt cork, for roles in a minstrel show, usually exaggerated for comic intent.

burlesque—Any broadly comic or satirical imitation

copyright—The exclusive right to the publication, production, or sale of a literary, musical, or artistic work granted by law for a definite period of years.

cottonwood—One of the poplars; a fast-growing tree used as fuel to stoke the steamboat furnaces. In the song "Nellie was a Lady," her grieving husband (the narrator) tells of "totin' cottonwood" and "floatin'" on the Mississippi, indicating his employment on a steamboat.

dialect—The form of spoken language peculiar to a region, community, social group, or occupational group. In the story, "blackface dialect" refers to the perceived dialect in the composer's imagination when writing minstrel songs.

febrile—Associated with fever, elevated body temperature; a description of Stephen's recurring illness.

free state—A state where slavery was unlawful. Because of the Fugitive Slave Law*, slaves were not really safe in the "free states" during the 1850s. They could be captured and returned to slavery. Canada was the refuge for blacks escaping slavery.

Fugitive Slave Law—A law that provided for the return of runaway slaves across state lines passed in 1793. An owner could recover his escaped slave by presenting proof of ownership to a magistrate. An order was then given for the arrest and return of the slave, who got no trial or the right to give evidence in his own behalf. Sometimes innocent (free) blacks were kidnapped and taken to the South as slaves. Since the law was abused, some states issued orders not to help in the recovery of fugitive slaves, and for many years, the law was not imposed. In the Compromise of 1850, the law was revived, imposing heavy penalties upon persons who aided a slave's escape or interfered with a slave's recovery.

gaiter—A strip of fabric covering the leg from the instep to either the ankle or the knee; an ankle-high shoe with elastic at the sides and no laces.

gay—Joyous and lively. The word is used in several of Stephen's songs and has the connotation of merriment.

indentured servant—A person bound by contract to work for another, usually for a certain period of time until his/her passage (trip to America) had been worked off or whatever other debt had been paid.

lithographic—Pertaining to the art or practice of writing on a flat stone or metal plate with a greasy substance, inking the surface and making paper impressions of the original. Some of the results were crude. Chromolithography came later. In this process, several colors and plates were used, and the effect was improved.

muse—The power regarded as inspiring a poet or artist to think or create.

paradox—A statement, proposition, or situation that seems to be absurd or contradictory but, in fact, is or may be true.

reciprocally—Refers to giving or feeling something mutually.

Social Orchestra—The "Social Orchestra," very common in the nineteenth century, included four or five instruments or less. Stephen's publication by that name was intended for such an orchestra providing dance and serenade music for the home. Except for the New York Philharmonic Society, which numbered about sixty players and played just a few times per year, no full orchestra existed in America during Stephen's era. The largest orchestras of twenty or thirty wind and string instruments accompanied operas and dramas.

stevedore—A person employed at loading and unloading ships

swan song—The last creative work of a person. Stephen wrote at least fifty songs after he wrote "Beautiful Dreamer," but since "Beautiful Dreamer" was not published until after he died, it serves here as a symbolic swan song.

syncopation—A rhythmic technique in music in which the accent is shifted to a weak beat of the bar

Taylor, Zachary—General Zachary Taylor was a hero of the Mexican War. The new territories acquired by the United States through the victory in Mexico would cause more controversy over the slavery situation. The question had to be settled whether the new states would be admitted to the Union as slave states or as free ones. Zachary Taylor, a large slaveholder, was elected president of the United States in 1849. He urged that California be admitted to the Union as a free state but did not support the compromise resolutions that several members of congress were trying to establish to restore harmony in the country. When Taylor died in office, Millard Fillmore became president. He was in favor of the Compromise of 1850 and helped push it through the Congress, delaying the civil war by ten years.

Temperance Movement—Members of the Temperance Movement took vows for total abstinence from alcoholic beverages. (Many members were not alcoholics.) The organizations were very strong in the nineteenth century and came about as a reaction to the problems of public drunkenness and the poverty resulting in families whose breadwinners were victims of alcoholism.

Underground Railroad—The Underground Railroad was not a railroad and was not underground. It was an informal system of helping runaway slaves escape to the Northern states and Canada to freedom. Railroad terms were used as code words. Runaways hid in "stations"—safe houses—along the route. "Conductors" provided shelter, supplies, and transportation.

Whig—A member of a certain American political party. The Whigs won the presidency with Zachary Taylor in 1849 but were losing power by 1856 and broke up into sectional groups over the question of slavery. Many Northern Whigs joined the new Republican Party, and many Southern Whigs joined the Democrats. By 1860, the remaining Whigs became part of the Constitutional Union Party.

Notes

1.   Austin, 61.

Chapter One

1.   Howard, 20.
2.   Ibid., 78.

Chapter Two

1.   Morneweck, Vol. 1,167.
2.   Howard, 103.
3.   Ibid., 113.
4.   Ibid., 106.

Chapter Six

1.   Deane Root. *The American Experience: Stephen Foster. video*

Chapter Seven

1.   Emerson, 195.

Chapter Twelve

1.   Emerson, 287.

Bibliography

Allen, Michael. *The Western Rivermen, 1763-1861: Ohio and Mississippi Boatmen and the Myth of the Alligator Horse.* Baton Rouge: Louisiana State University Press, 1990.

Austin, William W. *"Susanna," "Jeanie," and "The Old Folks At Home": The Songs of Stephen C. Foster from His Time to Ours.* Urbana and Chicago: University of Illinois Press, 1989.

Crawford, Richard. *America's Musical Life: A History.* New York: W. W. Norton and Company, 2001.

Emerson, Ken. *Doo-dah!: Stephen Foster and the Rise of American Popular Culture.* New York: Simon and Schuster, 1997.

Emerson, Ken, and Randall MacLowry. Stephen Foster, The American Experience. PBS, 2001. video

Foster Song Book. Original sheet music of forty songs by Stephen Collins Foster selected, with introduction and notes by Richard Jackson. New York: Dover Publication, 1974.

Fuld, James J. *The Book of World Famous Music,* 4th ed. New York: Dover Publications, 1995.

Hal Leonard Corporation. *Songs of Stephen Foster.* Original editions of thirty songs. Milwaukee: Hal Leonard.

Hitchcock, H. Wiley, and Stanley Sadie, eds. *New Grove Dictionary of American Music,* vol. 3. (New York, NY: Macmillan Press Limited, 1986), 650.

Howard, John Tasker. *Stephen Foster, America's Troubadour.* New York: Tudor Publishing Company, 1939.

Mahar, William J. *Behind the Burnt Cork Mask: Early Blackface Minstrelsy and Antebellum American Popular Culture.* Urbana and Chicago: University of Illinois Press, 1999.

Morneweck, Evelyn Foster. *Chronicles of Stephen Foster's Family.* 2 vols. Pittsburgh: University of Pittsburgh Press, 1944.

Songs, Compositions and Arrangements by Stephen Collins Foster, 1826-1864.

Produced by the Staff of Foster Hall and privately printed by Josiah Kirby Lilly. Indianapolis, Indiana: 1933.

Songs of Stephen Foster. Prepared especially for the armed forces by the staff of the Foster Hall Collection of the University of Pittsburgh. Pittsburgh: 1948.

Wade, Richard C. *The Urban Frontier: Pioneer Life in Early Pittsburgh.* Chicago: University of Chicago Press, 1959.

Walters, Raymond. *Stephen Foster, Youth's Golden Gleam: A Sketch of His Life and Background in Cincinnati, 1846-1850.* Princeton, NJ: Princeton University Press, 1936.

World Book Encyclopedia. USA: 1981

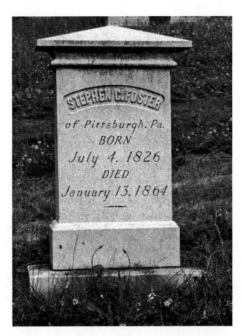

Stephen's grave in the Allegheny Cemetery.
Photo by Jerry Watts, June 2004

Stephen Foster, Retouched tintype. Courtesy of the Foster Hall
Collection, Center for American Music, University of Pittsburgh
Library System

Index

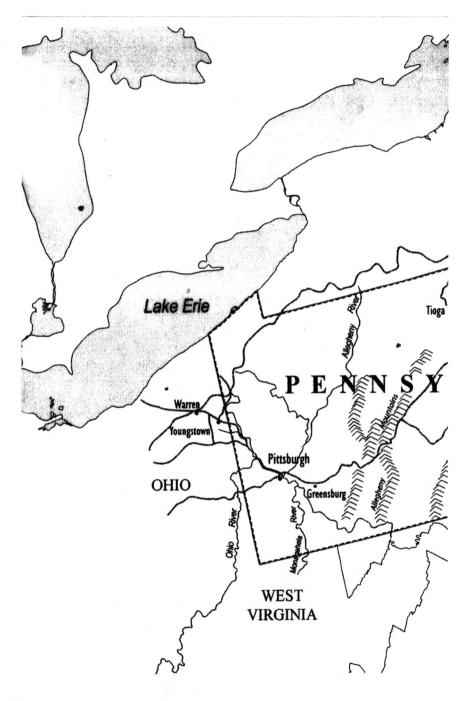

Map of Pennsylvania, showing
Bert Fontcuberta, The Map

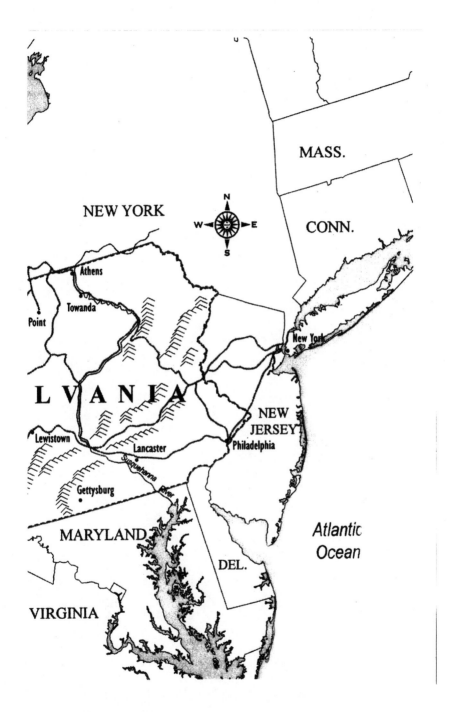

the Foster towns. Constructed by
Man, Covington, Louisiana.